A Planned Program for the Church Year

A Planned Program
for the
Church Year

Weldon Crossland

ABINGDON-COKESBURY PRESS
New York • Nashville

A PLANNED PROGRAM FOR THE CHURCH YEAR

SET UP, PRINTED, AND BOUND BY THE
PARTHENON PRESS, AT NASHVILLE,
TENNESSEE, UNITED STATES OF AMERICA

PREFACE

THIS book deals with what many church leaders regard as the most promising present-day trend in the life of the local church—a planned program for the coming year.

By carefully choosing their objectives for the year, by daringly setting their desired goals, by wisely selecting their new projects, and by confidently projecting their year's program in all areas of church life, churches find that they steadily advance in strength and service.

The plans and projects presented here rank among the most successful of those used by hundreds of churches and ministers of many denominations. They present a tried technique of long-range, unified planning that can be readily adapted to the size and needs of any church, large or small, rural or urban.

Basic in all church-wide planning for the church year is the lay-ministerial partnership, with trained laymen bearing the largest possible share of the administrative responsibility for the activities of the congregation.

Because the accent of this volume throughout is on the over-all planned program of objectives, emphases, and projects rather than on detailed methods, brevity has been deliberately cultivated. An entire volume could have been written on each one of these chapters.

Every church, of any size in any communion anywhere, that has planned its work and worked its plan on a twelve-month basis has entered a new era of vastly enriched life and broadened Christian service.

WELDON CROSSLAND

CONTENTS

CHAPTER 1

How to Plan a Church-wide Program

BASIC PRINCIPLES

1. The work of every church is of such supreme importance as to deserve the most careful, long-range planning.
2. Any minister of any church of any size, anywhere, can lead his congregation in outlining its program on a twelve-month basis.
3. All areas of church life and work must be included in the projected plans.
4. The calendar and objectives of the denomination to which the church belongs must be woven into the total program.
5. The program should be co-operatively worked out by the official committees and groups of the church in consultation with their minister.
6. A Church-wide Planning Conference of all church officials and leaders must be called to discuss and improve the proposed plans.
7. A three-year or five-year plan of continuous growth and expansion possesses high value for any church.

INCREASED thousands of progressive ministers and growing churches are today planning their work and working their plans on a long-range basis through what has come to be called "A Planned Program for the Church Year." These churches range in size from sixty members to over three thousand, and are found in rural, urban, and metropolitan communities. Without exception they report that church life has been unified and strengthened, that church interest and loyalty have grown, and that the range of Christian service has been enlarged and its quality enriched.

What is a planned program? What are its chief values? What areas of church life does it include? How does a church set about outlining a program for the year ahead?

"A Planned Program for the Church Year" is a comprehensive outline of the chief objectives, plans, and activities of the local church in all its varied departments, co-operatively prepared by the church leaders and the minister in advance for the next twelve months. It is church planning on a yearly basis, by which desired goals are set, sound plans are laid, and a calendar of the chief events of the church year is prepared.

Long-term planning has for decades been common practice in the world of successful business. Railroads, telephone companies, and automobile manufacturers through their research departments project their plans five or ten years that they may anticipate public tastes and needs and exploit the sales opportunities that face them. "The firm that does not look ahead will fail," represents the unanimous judgment of able businessmen.

In ecclesiastical life some churches have for centuries followed the Christian year in their services of worship. The holy days of the Christian calendar, the vestments of the priest or minister, and even the color of the altar decorations at certain seasons conform to a fixed schedule, while the collects, responses, Bible readings, confessions, and prayers are specified "for the day."

At the higher levels of the national denominational boards of education, missions, youth work, and women's activities one finds an amazing amount of long-range planning. Curriculums for the church school, mission study courses, and evangelism schedules are outlined months in advance that texts may be written and promotional materials prepared. Probably the most comprehensive denominational planned program is *The Presbyterian Plan Book,* issued annually in July by the Presbyterian Church, U. S. A., to promote the educational, missionary, evangelistic, and other phases of the growing religious life of the local church.

Aside from estimating the annual budget, the programs of tens of thousands of Protestant churches are like Creation before the Spirit of God moved upon it—without form, and void; and darkness is on the face of it. These churches live in a hand-to-mouth extempore manner. They are "guesswork churches." Their plans lack perspective, continuity, and effectiveness. They are opportunist churches, using techniques that are immature and catch as catch can. To use an analogy of the golf course, their stance is careless, they fail to keep their eyes on the ball, they do not follow through, and they turn in an extremely poor score at the end of the Christian year.

Avoiding both the stereotyped dullness of the static church year and the confused chaos of the planless church year, the worthy church will choose rather a dynamic church year by intelligently choosing objectives and carefully laying plans for all departments of its Christian life.

Recognize the values of long-range planning. Churches that have planned their work and work their plan on a yearly basis have found these eight chief advantages:

1. All the work of the church is vastly broadened and improved.

2. Each chairman sees his kingdom task in terms of a well-rounded, twelve-month program of activity rather than from the standpoint of a single event. As he visualizes the needs and opportunities of his committee or group for the year ahead, he takes a more serious view of his responsibilities and will prepare more adequately.

3. All leaders of the church become acquainted with the total program of the church through the Church-wide Planning Conference. This becomes an education in churchmanship.

4. All phases of church life are unified and integrated. Competing or conflicting dates are easily adjusted while plans are still in the formative stage.

5. The leaders and members of the church gain a sense of going forward together as they see the unity and continuity that come from intelligent foresight and unhurried planning. Each year builds on the experience of the previous one.

6. The monthly meetings of the congregation, session, or board are much more interesting as standing and special committees report on past activities and future plans.

7. Laymen more readily take their fair share of the responsibility for the administrative load of the church when they have played a prominent role in planning it.

8. The minister is freed from much of the distraction of committee meetings and daily administrative detail and is able to devote himself more fully to those professional duties which only he can perform.

If any pastor should exclaim, "What a lot of work!" let him know that the time required to plan a year's total program is about one third of that involved in any other method. Hundreds of hours of the minister's valuable time are saved. If anyone should suggest, "A large church can plan ahead but a small church cannot," let him be assured that a three-point circuit in Alabama and a small church of a hundred members in Michigan adapt this planning technique to their situations and needs as effectively as do churches of more than two thousand members. If a minister objects, "I don't like a program that is too stereotyped;

I want to be free," let him be reminded that since the planned program has been created by him and his people, they have the right to change it at will. And if some pastor asserts, "Some ministers can do this while others cannot," let him be warned that such a statement is contradicted by the experience of all who have used it. Planning on a yearly basis can be achieved in any church by any minister anywhere.

Outline an over-all procedure. In all phases of church-wide planning the minister plays the leading role as counselor, guide, and leader. He must create confidence and kindle enthusiasm as the leader of the leaders of the church. He must first think through each major phase of the movements that culminate in the Church-wide Planning Conference. He must thoroughly believe in the philosophy of church-wide planning and must adapt it in scope and schedule to his own church. He will tentatively list the dates into which the successive features of the unfolding movement will fit. One minister whose church holds its planning conference about June 10 recommends the following schedule:

February 1: Present the Church-wide Planning Conference plan to the congregation for discussion and approval.

March 1: Elect or appoint committee chairmen and members as well as heads of organizations for the coming year.

April 1-30: Interview all chairmen and leaders individually.

May 1-20: Hold meetings of all committees and groups to plan their year's work.

May 21: Deadline date for all reports and recommendations.

May 22-27: Make duplicated copies of these reports.

May 29: Mail the copies of the reports with a covering letter to all officials, committee chairmen, and committee members for study.

June 10: Hold the Church-wide Planning Conference.

The first step is to *win the approval of officials and members*. The wise minister will discuss the planned program idea with three or four influential leaders in order to secure their co-operation before he lays the plan before the official body of his church. The superintendent of the church school, the chairman of the finance committee, and the president of the women's guild will readily approve as the minister describes the purpose of long-range planning, explains the techniques of the planning conference, and states the advantages of co-operative counsel by the leaders of the church.

Then the minister will *recommend a Church-wide Planning Conference*. He will explain to the church officials that thousands of churches of all sizes are now successfully using "A Planned Program for the Church Year" with its slogan "Plan Your Work and Work Your Plan"; that each committee or group in the church will prepare a report and recommendations concerning what ought to be done during the coming year in their field; that copies of these reports will be laid before the official body of the church for discussion; and that wherever tried, this method has strengthened and broadened the program of the church. As pastor he will then recommend that a committee of three or five be appointed to work out this plan with the minister. After discussion and approval, the planning committee, under the chairmanship of the minister, will proceed to set the date for the planning conference and to make careful preparations for it.

The next step is to *choose committees and organization*

leaders. They should be selected early in the spring so that they may plan the work for the coming year while the life of the church is still at high tide. Because of the fact that a large majority of chairmen are re-elected annually, there will be no confusion in planning ahead. When a chairman is retiring, he will gladly give his co-operation and suggestions to his successor.

The minister should *counsel with each leader or chairman.* His soundest strategy is to persuade his laymen to assume active leadership in planning and in taking the responsibility for putting those plans into operation. The foolish minister will write out a full report for each chairman or leader, in this way stultifying any practical and creative ideas the chairman may have, as well as sapping his initiative and enthusiasm. The wise minister will draw out the chairman's suggestions. The rich resource material for a planned program is usually drawn from the following sources: (1) the work of the church during the previous year; (2) the needs of the congregation; (3) the new opportunities for service before the church; (4) the recommendations of the denomination concerning projects and dates; (5) the plans of interdenominational agencies for the observance of such events as Christian Education Week, World Communion Sunday, and the Week of Prayer; and (6) the suggestions of the committee members and the minister.

Make each committee meeting an adventure in co-operative planning. Since the chairman has clarified his own thinking and knows what is in his pastor's mind, he is prepared to take active and vigorous leadership of the meeting of his committee. He may invite his committee to his own home for this important evening. He will encourage the pooling of their ideas by stating the items of the order of business in question form, such as: What were the most successful features of our committee's work last year? Where did we fail to do as well as we should? What new features might we add to our program for the coming year? What are other churches doing in this field? What does our denomination recommend? Which of the features which we have discussed tonight should be put into our program for the coming year? Shall we ask our chairman and minister to put these suggestions in the form of a report and recommendation that they may be laid before the Church-wide Planning Conference? Once the aims, emphases, and projects have been determined by the committee, it is a simple matter to formulate and type these in compact form.

It is important to *distribute copies of all these reports* to all leaders and officials, with a covering letter of invitation to attend the planning conference. The usual order of arrangement of material in the planning conference booklet is as follows:

Chief achievements of the closing year
Major objectives for the coming year
The Christian year in worship and preaching
Midweek service of Bible study and fellowship
Communion services
Baptismal services
Lenten and Holy Week services
Board of education
Church school
Youth activities
Women's organizations
Board of trustees
Official committees
Other groups

These reports will require about eight pages for a smaller church and from fifteen to thirty for a larger one.

Under an attractive cover, bearing perhaps a stenciled drawing of the church, these reports are stapled in booklet form.

Conduct the Church-wide Planning Conference. The minister of course will preside over the conference, which may be held during the evening or as a Saturday or Sunday afternoon retreat. After asking God's rich blessing on the church and its leadership, he will explain its purpose and the procedure of the gathering. He will encourage and urge everyone present to share in the discussion with constructive and critical comment, as each section of the report is presented.

After the minister has read "the achievements" and "the objectives" and has invited full discussion of these, he will present his outline of the services and sermon subjects he has chosen for the Christian year. He will indicate the chief special days, the sermon series he has included, and the other sermon topics on which he expects to preach. He will make it clear that these plans and themes, like all others laid before the conference, are tentative and subject to change, and that he covets, as every chairman does, the frank judgment of everyone present.

Each chairman or organization head will then be asked to read or scan and to explain his report and recommendation. He will ask for the opinions of everyone present, with the assurance that all of these will be laid before his committee and in so far as is desirable will be included in the work of the year. In one planning conference sixty-seven different suggestions were offered. Many ministers close the conference with a service of dedication.

Announce the plans to the congregation. Every member should be informed of the total program for the year ahead. One minister takes an entire morning service for this purpose, preaching on churchmanship in terms of every member sharing in the work of the church. Another pastor mails a copy of the revised plans to every family. One prints an eight-page folder covering the services, meetings, and events of each three-month period, while others also encourage each organization to print or duplicate a program of its own for use in increasing interest and attendance.

Churches everywhere that have used the planning conference technique have found that their aims have been clarified, their methods improved, and their range of Christian service steadily expanded.

Ministers have discovered that their ministry has been remade, their usefulness multiplied, and their congregations enlarged and unified as they lead their laymen in planning their church work and working their church plans.

CHAPTER 2

How to Choose the Major Objectives

BASIC PRINCIPLES

1. The supreme aim of every church is that of bringing men to Christ and revealing Christ to men in all his redeeming love.
2. Major emphases and goals should be set annually by every church.
3. These objectives should include those recommended by the denominational and interdenominational organizations to which each church belongs.
4. The goals and quotas which a church sets for itself will strongly influence its growth and achievement.
5. The successes of the closing year should be listed in the planning conference program as an encouraging challenge to church leaders as they face the new year.
6. A study of the unmet religious needs of the church and the community will reveal many Christian service opportunities.

WHAT a destination and a chosen road are to the traveler, aims and objectives are to the local church and to the minister who serves it. These give added meaning and high strategy to the Christian program. These unify and synchronize its varied activities, welding a number of scattered detachments into an advancing army of the Lord. They release and direct the energies of pastor and people into kingdom channels.

Because the church is a divine institution, established by Jesus Christ, and because, as the fellowship of the saints and the family of God, it is the most important

21

organization in the community, it deserves the most careful planning that the mind of man, illumined by the
Spirit of God, can give it.

List the aims of every Christian church. Most Christians
would agree that the following rank high among the
important duties of any church:

To preach the good news of Jesus Christ, the Son of God
To witness the Christian faith before the world
To encourage individuals to live the Christlike life
To develop growing Christian personalities
To worship God and to do his will
To persuade individuals to loving loyalty to Jesus Christ
To educate growing persons in Christian faith and fellowship
To indoctrinate concerning Christian truths and convictions
To Christianize all individual and social life
To challenge sinners to repentance
To transform society through the power and love of Jesus
    Christ
To serve mankind
To cultivate world-wide Christian brotherhood
To comfort those in sorrow and to help those in need
To inspire youth to sacrificial Christian living
To administer the sacraments
To provide Christian fellowship in worship, friendship, and
    service

The divine commission to the Christian church includes
these and all other objectives that are in harmony with
the purposes of God.

There are at least these four major areas in which any
church with a well-rounded program of Christian service
should seek to carry out the above aims:

Worship and preaching, which would include public services,
    private worship, preaching, church loyalty and membership,

sacred music, and the administration of the sacraments

Christian education, which comprises the church school in its broadest interpretation as the total educational ministry of the church, the board of education, Christian literature, the whole range of youth interests and activities, and the Christian training and nurture of children

Christian fellowship, which would embrace all church social life, as well as fellowship with other churches in common tasks

Christian service to the community and to the world through sharing, missions, evangelism, Christian social action of community life, charity, and outreach

There are important current trends in American church life which should not be overlooked. Any church that would serve the present age must give careful study to major changes in emphases and techniques that are contributing so much to the growing richness and adequacy of the Christian program of the local church. Among these chief trends which are constructively influencing church thought and life are the following:

More careful long-range planning of the work of the local church

The working out of a united church strategy

The exaltation of the Christian church and the cultivation of churchmanship

Active interchurch co-operation on local, county, state, national, and international levels

Interchurch organic union

A renewed interest in Christian theology

More adequately trained ministers

Longer pastorates

More beautiful and useful church edifices

More impressive services of worship

Greatly improved Christian education

Emphasis on Christian vocation and Christian life service
An aggressive, inclusive evangelism
More adequate membership training and indoctrination
Daily devotions through prayer and Bible reading
The dynamic application of Christian principles to social problems
An awareness and appreciation of the Protestant, evangelical Christian heritage

These basic trends, fused in a united Christian strategy, assure a bright future for the Protestant Christian churches.

Consider denominational and interchurch plans. Nation-wide program building on a twelve-month basis is coming to be the accepted practice of nearly all the leading communions in the United States. These projected plans never seek to regiment or stereotype the local church, but rather to place before it the worthiest aims and the most effective plans as formulated by the national boards and leaders. For example, the first four-year plan adopted by The Methodist Church at the end of World War II emphasized reconstruction, missions, evangelism, and Christian education, while the second four-year plan stresses "Our Faith," "Our Church," "Our Ministry," and "Our Missions." Each minister will want to use the denominational church year as recommended by his communion as the framework of the twelve-month program of the local church.

No local church program could be either adequate or Christian that did not give a large place also to the activities and interests which the Christian churches have in common. United interchurch action has repeatedly proved its superior effectiveness in many areas of Christian endeavor. In union there is added strength for every local church that wholeheartedly participates.

Any church program would be glaringly incomplete if it did not include either in co-operation with other churches or alone the observance of such special days and seasons as Reformation Sunday, the Week of Prayer, One Great Hour, the Lenten period, Holy Week services—including, when acceptable, the three-hour Good Friday service—and Easter Day. Such interchurch movements as community surveys, visitation evangelism crusades, and simultaneous financial campaigns for raising all church budgets have repeatedly proved that in union there is increased value and strength for the local church. Co-operating churches everywhere find that one of the most valued by-products of united action is to be found in the exchange of ideas, objectives, and methods. Ecclesiastical cross-fertilization produces sometimes thirty, sometimes sixty, and sometimes a hundredfold return to the individual church.

Study your church's needs and opportunities. Some congregations have lived so long with stained or dingy walls, dog-eared hymnals, a ragged carpet, unsatisfactory music, a diminishing youth group, and a small congregation of older people, that they would be amazed and shocked if they could know how unnecessary and intolerable these conditions appear to nonmembers. Vast harm is done to the reputation of the church and to its relation to the public because it fails to see and meet many evident needs.

Probably the best way to compel a congregation to meet its more pressing needs is to ask such pertinent questions as these:

Why do we have such small congregations?
Why do we have such a small church school, with so many children, youth, and adults all around us?

How can we cultivate more friendliness after our church services?

What can we do to make the exterior and interior of our church more attractive?

Do we need more younger men in positions of official leadership?

How much more money would be required to do the things we ought to do for our church and its program?

Are we following the financial plans recommended by our denomination?

Could we double the amount we now give to missions?

Are we losing our young married people because we have no class or fellowship for them?

What is our program for youth, and how can we reach more young people?

What are we doing to serve our community?

One church revolutionized its entire program and life by inviting one of its state officials to spend a week end in studying the strengths, the weaknesses, and the opportunities before the congregation. His impartial analysis and friendly counsel opened a new era of growth and service for that congregation.

Vision and clear thinking on the part of the minister, and faith and devotion on the part of the laity, are necessary if a church is to embrace the almost unlimited opportunities that face it. One church determined to double its church membership and attendance over a four-year period, as well as to increase the number of pledgers by one hundred per cent. It succeeded. Another church transformed its unsightly basement into a youth center, where young people gathered every evening in the week for fellowship, fun, interest and hobby groups, meeting each Sunday in a great worship service. Another church dou-

bled the number of boys and girls in its children's department by calling in the homes of the families within three
city blocks of the church. Another church brought well-
known preachers to the community on the Wednesday
evenings of Lent. A neighborhood church organized and
trained more than two hundred children and young people in four excellent choirs. Another church, with a
nucleus of four young couples, created a young adult
fellowship that numbered eighty at the end of the year.

Any new project requires careful planning, wise selection of leadership, a timetable of unfolding activities, and
an inspiring program of fellowship and service.

Review the past year's achievements. The continuing
program of the worth-while things any church is doing will
provide most of the framework within which church
leaders will choose their objectives for the first year of its
planning. While entirely new and untried projects should
be included whenever desirable, most of the objectives
chosen will be found to fit into the areas of worship, Christian education, fellowship, and service already being cultivated. A list of the important achievements of the past
year will serve as an incentive to wider service for the
coming one.

Churches of various denominations, ranging in membership from fifty-seven to over two thousand, have supplied
the following selected examples of worthy past-year achievements from their lists:

The Sunday school increased 22 per cent in average attend-
ence over the previous year.

Forty-four new members were received into the fellowship
of the church, an increase of 12 per cent for the year.

An endowment gift of $5,000 was received.

A Younger Married Class was organized by five couples. The membership is now thirty-two.

Our mortgage indebtedness of $17,500 was reduced $6,000 this year, with an annual saving in interest of $300.

A children's choir was organized with a membership of twenty-eight.

The Interchurch Evangelistic Crusade in which we shared resulted in 112 new members for our church.

Twenty men and women have been trained for evangelistic calling.

New hymnals were provided for our church services.

Over $103,000 was promised in two-year pledges toward our new community house. To date $46,370 has been paid in cash.

We burned our mortgage on Palm Sunday, making our church debt free for the first time in thirty-five years.

Any church can list five or six notable successes in its life and work as a stimulus to greater service for the coming year.

Select challenging goals for the future. Among the major objectives chosen by churches, large and small, in many communions are the following:

- To increase every-Sunday church attendance by urging the duty of regular worship by every member of the church
- To launch a Church Loyalty Crusade, during the month of October, opening with World Communion Sunday
- To present Jesus Christ in service, sermon, and personal life as God's solution to the moral problems and the spiritual needs of today

To reclaim indifferent church members to a renewed loyalty to the church

To secure the attendance of 400 of our 492 members at the sacrament of Holy Communion

- To enlarge and improve the musical program of the church by organizing a children's choir and a youth choir

. To encourage daily Bible reading and prayer in every home by every member of the church

. To increase the membership and average attendance of the church school 25 per cent each year for the next three years

. To secure a sound-motion picture projector so that our church may present religious films

· To stress leadership education and the training of present and prospective teachers

. To conduct a daily vacation church school next summer

· To develop a great church night program on one Friday evening each month so as to include children as well as adults

· To organize two married couples' classes, one for younger couples and another for older couples

. To expand the youth program in its Sunday and weekday activities, with the aim of serving twice as many young people as we now do

· To encourage young people to give serious consideration to devoting their lives to Christian service

. To lift to higher levels the spirit of Christian fellowship and friendliness in our church

· To increase youth participation in the services and life of our church

To keep in closer touch with our young people who are attending college

· To stress Christian missions as the most helpful and permanent bond of international brotherhood

To conduct a house-to-house survey of the community in co-operation with other churches

· To expand the program of work of the Women's Guild through calling and service

· To cultivate Christian stewardship of means, time, and life

To establish an endowment fund and to encourage the giving of gifts and bequests to it

To enroll one fifth of our membership as tithing stewards

To emphasize the duty and privilege of pledging and giving
   regularly to Christ's work through the church

To repaint the exterior of the church this year and to redeco-
   rate the interior next year

To secure needed equipment, such as tower chimes, hearing
   aids, and a new organ, as gifts or memorials

To remodel the chancel of the church to make it more worship-
   ful and attractive

To encourage every boy and girl from the children's and youth
   departments to make a pledge to the church

To call on and welcome all newcomers in the community

Probably more than a score of additional objectives suited
to the needs of the church can be listed by any congregation under the guidance of its minister.

Long-range objectives should be chosen, even though
detailed plans are made only for the year ahead. The
Master once said that the children of this world are often
wiser in their generation than the children of light. His
comment would seem to apply to the several Five-Year
Plans of Communist Russia as compared with the lack of
any long-range strategy on the part of most Christian
churches.

The number of churches, large and small, that have
worked out three-year or four-year or five-year plans is
growing to be an impressive one. Many of them have
appointed a five-year planning committee of seven members, dividing the areas of study among the committee
members into these subdivisions: (1) worship, membership, and missions; (2) Christian education; (3) young
people's activities; (4) women's work; (5) religion in
the home; (6) finances and endowment; (7) social life and
community service. These committees make an intensive

study of the present organization, activities, and religious needs of the membership. Their next step is to discover the program of objectives and work of the most successful churches in the community as well as in the state and throughout the nation. Said one minister, "Never have I seen a group of lay men and women, representing thirty-five families in our church, more keenly interested in and more deeply stirred by the challenge of any worthwhile task than were these committee members."

When the achievements of one five-year plan were checked against the objectives recommended, it was found that 91 per cent of them had been reached. These included the organization of four new church-school classes, the formation of two choirs for children and young people, the liquidation of the debt, the increase of permanent endowment from $1,000 to $31,000, and an increase of $2,000 annually to missions.

Intelligent, long-range planning by the leaders of any Christian church will pay dividends rich beyond any congregation's fondest hopes.

Try it!

SPECIMEN COMMITTEE REPORTS

Achievements of the Closing Year, pages 130-31
Objectives for the Coming Year, page 131
Building Committee, page 149

CHAPTER 3

How to Outline a Year's Sermon Subjects

BASIC PRINCIPLES

1. The public services of worship and preaching outrank in importance any other service rendered by the church.
2. The sermon offers the minister his greatest religious task and opportunity of the week.
3. Every minister should select his sermon themes for a three-, six-, or twelve-month period, with the expectation of changing any chosen subject for a more timely one if desirable.
4. Long-range sermonic planning improves preaching, avoids repetition, saves time, and permits the accumulation of material over a period of months for each sermon.
5. The special days and seasons of the Christian year afford outstanding opportunities for great preaching.
6. The excellence of the sermon and the service largely determines the size of the congregation and the regularity of its attendance.

Any minister can become a more effective preacher if he will intelligently plan and faithfully work at this God-given task. If he habitually comes to Saturday afternoon or evening, having asked himself a dozen times during the week with increasing anxiety, "Oh, what shall I preach about next Sunday?" his sermons will be ordinary, repetitious, monotonous, and inadequately prepared. If he confidently begins on Monday morning with the accumulated references, illustrations, poems, and thoughts concerning the great theme he carefully chose months ago, he will, as a good minister of Jesus Christ, build his reading, his meditation, and his insight into an inspiring sermon.

From the lips of seven ministers who choose their sermon subjects three months or more in advance come these enthusiastic comments concerning the advantages of long-range sermonic planning:

I save a vast amount of time. I can remember weeks, before I began planning my preaching program, when I spent more time choosing a sermon subject than I did on preparing the sermon itself.

My preaching has become stronger and more interesting because I now have a well-balanced range of subjects.

My sermons now are not guilty of monotony and repetition, whatever other faults they may have. They cover a wider range of great religious themes.

I accumulate material for my sermons across the months, especially during my summer vacation. I file the illustrations, poems, ideas, and clippings in the letter-size folder which I make for each sermon subject.

The members of my congregation approve and applaud my long-range choice of sermon subjects. They know they get better sermons on greater themes.

While I change about one in seven sermon subjects I have chosen for the year in the interest of some unexpected or timely theme, I find I can more helpfully fit the timely into the timeless themes of my preaching.

A more unified service of worship and preaching can be planned by my director of music and myself when we know these sermon themes for the next three months. He selects and rehearses appropriate music for five or six weeks in advance.

How can this sermonic planning be done? How does one start? What successive steps do experienced ministers take in outlining their pulpit subjects for the year that lies ahead?

Select a theme for the year. It is a growing custom among ministers to organize their ministry of preaching for the year around some unifying idea. They feel that to lead their people thoroughly through some area of Christian truth is more helpful than to try to cover all phases of truth in fifty-two Sundays. They prefer to visit one country in their twelve-month sermonic journey instead of becoming breathless globe-trotters. Examples of these comprehensive themes, suggested by some denomination or used by a minister, are the following:

> Building Anew with Christ
> Christ for Every Life and All of Life
> The Place of Religion in the World Today
> Forward with Jesus Christ
> Personal Religion
> The Greatest Texts in the Bible
> Everlasting Values in a World of Change
> The New Church for the New World
> Our Faith (developing the theme month by month
>   of faith in God, Christ, the Holy Spirit, the Bible,
>   love, prayer, immortality, the Kingdom of God,
>   etc.)

Over a period of three to five years under this plan scores of great sermons will have been preached on notable themes to the enrichment and deepening of the Christian life of the congregation.

Build upon the special Sundays. Take twelve sheets of paper, marking one for each month, fill in the dates of the Sundays of the calendar year, and place opposite the appropriate dates those special Sundays which you wish to observe, such as Labor Sunday, Christian Education Sunday, World Communion Sunday, Thanksgiving Sunday, Christmas Sunday, the Sundays in Lent, Easter Day, and Mother's Day. A fairly complete list of the special Sundays commonly observed will be found on page 45. This outline may be as simple or as elaborate as the custom of the church or the desire of the minister may dictate. But in nearly every communion one discovers a growing practice of using the chief days of the Christian year as the spiritual framework for both preaching and worship. Using the date of Easter in the following twenty-four-year calendar as a starting point, one can easily determine the dates of Palm Sunday, Ash Wednesday, Pentecost, and other special days:

1952—Apr. 13	1960—Apr. 17	1968—Apr. 14
1953—Apr. 5	1961—Apr. 2	1969—Apr. 6
1954—Apr. 18	1962—Apr. 22	1970—Mar. 29
1955—Apr. 10	1963—Apr. 14	1971—Apr. 11
1956—Apr. 1	1964—Mar. 29	1972—Apr. 2
1957—Apr. 21	1965—Apr. 18	1973—Apr. 22
1958—Apr. 6	1966—Apr. 10	1974—Apr. 14
1959—Mar. 29	1967—Mar. 26	1975—Mar. 30

Though the theme of each of the recurring special days of the Christian calendar is perennial, the spirit and events of any given period will aid the preacher in treating them in a timely and appropriate way. Having before him the sermon subjects of the two or three previous years, he may select a portion of the theme with which he has not dealt. One minister selected the following themes for his Christian Education Sunday sermons across three years: "The Fine Art of Growing," "Christ, the Supreme Teacher," "Creative Christian Character." Another minister for his successive thanksgiving sermon themes chose "The Goodness of God," "The Grace of Gratitude," "Thanks for Everything." With his past subjects as a background any minister can wisely determine the varied sermon subjects he desires for the special Sundays.

The six Sundays in Lent leading up to Easter Day offer the preacher his greatest sermonic opportunity of the year. Christians in nearly all communions are increasingly sensitive to the obligations and opportunities of the Lenten period. At no time in the year are they more receptive to guidance in self-examination, self-denial, self-development, and growth in Christlikeness. What an opportunity every preacher has for presenting the glorious truths of our religion, the radiant realities by which we live! Every sermon should be an inspiring one on one of the greatest of themes.

If any timid pastor fears that he might be guilty of repetition, let him be comforted with the assurance that the sermonic memories of his parishioners are rather short, and that the number of sermons that can be preached on any great theme is very long. One Iowa minister, under the Lenten-Easter title of "Fundamentals of an Enlarging Faith," preached on successive Sundays on these seven themes: "A Friendlier God," "A Diviner Christ," "A Nobler Church," "A Larger Kingdom," "A Worthier Prayer," "A Greater Victory," and "A Richer Immortality." Another, preaching on the general theme "What Christ Does for Men Today," chose these topics: "Christ Forgives Sin," "Christ Redeems Men," "Christ Kindles Hope," "Christ Provides Power," "Christ Reveals God," "Christ Gives Victory" (Palm Sunday), and "Christ Conquers Death" (Easter).

Many churches, either alone or in co-operation with

other congregations in the neighborhood, secure the ablest possible guest preachers from neighboring cities for the Wednesdays or Thursdays of Lent. When widely advertised, these services through their freewill offering will not only cover all expenses and serve the community but will also be a stimulating challenge to each minister to better preaching in his Sunday services.

Fill in with series of sermons to fit the weeks between special Sundays. A succession of several sermons on a great general theme holds far more interest for any congregation than most ministers realize. Laymen value highly the thoroughness with which a subject is treated when it is divided and developed in a workmanlike way. The continuity of interest also makes for a greater regularity in church attendance. Ministers have found that between the special Sundays of the Christian year several groups of sermons fit admirably into the sermonic framework. Among the series that have been used by preachers of many communions are the following:

The Apostles' Creed—under the general affirmation I Believe!
The Lord's Prayer
Christian Habits—including prayer, stewardship, faith, service, and church attendance
The Ten Commandments—which offer an arresting challenge to the moral relativity of today
Psalms That Inspire and Bless
Sermons from the Sermon on the Mount
Helps to Happiness—based on the Beatitudes
Victorious Personalities
Modern Saints—such as Schweitzer, Kagawa, and Grenfell
The Parables of Jesus
Christ and Present-Day Needs
Sermons on Poise and Power

Illustrated Missionary Travelogues—presented through colored
  slides and motion pictures
Great Men of the Old and New Testaments
Great Women of the Old and New Testaments
Sermons from Great Books of the Bible—such as Job, Isaiah,
  Acts, and Romans

The field of biblical themes and characters offers an
inexhaustible source of inspiring sermon topics for single
sermons or for series. The great characters of the Old
Testament, the heroic personalities of the New Testament,
choice texts from the Bible, and books like Job, Acts, and
Romans provide a never-failing list of stimulating themes.
When a minister adds to this impressive list those current
subjects on which he feels a strong urge to preach, he
will find that he has more sermon topics than he can possibly use in any twelve-month period.

Coin attractive titles. The central idea or message of
every sermon must be stated in a short, descriptive, challenging way if it is to have the pulling power of good
publicity. A sermon subject need not be either bizarre or
dull. The good news of the Son of God has a right to be
stated in such a manner that men in large numbers will
desire to hear it proclaimed. State the basic idea of each
sermon in five different ways as accurately, vigorously,
winsomely, and interestingly as you possibly can, and
from this list select the best one for its honored place
among your year's titles.

Any preaching schedule projected for a three-month,
six-month, or twelve-month period must be altered as
taste and necessity require. It must be adjustable and
elastic, for no minister is the slave of a thing he has
created. If one feels strongly moved by the Holy Spirit or

some less divine influence to preach on a subject other than the one he has unhurriedly selected some months before, it is of course his right to do so. Let him steadily improve his sermon themes throughout the year.

Gather material across the months by making a letter-size folder or large envelope for each sermon subject. By planning ahead any minister can easily accumulate a large amount of useful sermon material—subjects, poems, illustrations, quotations, and references—that will prove invaluable in the preparation of each sermon.

An indispensable aid to long-range planning, as well as to weekly sermon preparation, is a simple, usable filing system. Most filing plans are unnecessarily elaborate, and are inclined to break down or fall into disuse because they are so complicated. The test of any filing system is the rapidity and completeness with which it enables the minister to place before him all the material on a given subject to be found in his library.

Among the many cataloguing techniques I have seen is a simple, elastic system which enables one to place on his desk every poem, every illustration, every quotation, every article, and every sermon in his library, on any of a hundred or more different subjects, *and to do so in less than five minutes.* One need waste no time vainly asking himself, "Where in the world is that article or poem I saw? It's just the thing I need for this sermon!" The following outline indicates the indexing, classification, and equipment used:

1. Type the titles of sermons in books and magazines across the top of slips of paper—four by six inches or whatever size you habitually use—*in duplicate,* with the key number of the book or the name and date of the magazine, the page, and the text. For example, the title of the third sermon in Ralph W. Sockman's book *The Higher Happi-*

ness is listed as follows: "The Most Misunderstood Virtue, S21g, page 61, Matt. 5:5." A sermon in *The Pulpit* by Reuben K. Youngdahl is listed: "It Can Happen to You, Pulpit, Feb. 1950, page 38, Matt. 17:20." The key number of the book by Sockman, "S21g," is arrived at easily in the following manner: (*a*) Arrange all the books of sermons in your library in alphabetical order as to authors. (*b*) Write in white ink on the visible back of each book the initial letter of the surname of each author. (*c*) Assign an identifying number to each author, skipping some numbers to permit the inclusion of new authors later, so that these numbers will read for the "S" authors "S1," "S3," "S5," "S7," etc. (*d*) Where there is more than one book by an author, identify these several books with small letters of the alphabet in the order in which they were published, as follows for seven books by Sockman: "S21a," "S21b," and on through "S21g."

2. File these two duplicate sermon title slips in two files: (*a*) *according to the books of the Bible,* so that you will have a complete list of sermons on a given text; and (*b*) *according to subjects* of the sermons, so that you will have a complete list of all the sermons on a given subject. The following list of subjects, as used by some ministers, may be reduced or expanded as desired:

Advent	Builders	Christmas	Companion-
Age	Burdens	Church	ship
Appreciation	Challenge	Church	Confidence
Aspiration	Character	History	Conscience
Baptism	Children	Citizenship	Contentment
Beauty	Children of	Comfort	Courage
Bible	God	Common	Creed
Books	Christ	Things	Cross
Brotherhood	Christianity		Daily Living

Decision
Discipleship
Duty
Easter
Education
Evangelism
Experience
Faith
Fathers
Fear
Fellowship
Fidelity
Forgiveness
Foundations
Freedom
Friendship
Giving
God
God's Care
God's Immanence
God's Love
Gospel
Grace
Gratitude
Guidance
Happiness
Heaven
Holy Spirit

Home
Hope
Humanity
Humility
Immortality
Influence
Inspiration
Kindness
Kingdom of God
Labor
Law
Lent
Life
Light
Loneliness
Lord's Supper
Love
Loyalty
Materialism
Memorial Day
Mercy
Miracles
Miscellaneous
Missions
Morals
Mothers

Music
Nature
New Day
Obedience
Opportunity
Parables
Patience
Patriotism
Peace and War
Pentecost
Perseverance
Poverty
Power
Prayer
Preaching
Protestantism
Purity
Race Relations
Religion
Responsibility
Rest
Revelation
Rewards
Riches
Righteousness

Sacrifice
Saints
Salvation
Science
Self-Control
Selfishness
Service
Sin
Sorrow
Soul
Stewardship
Strength
Success
Suffering
Sympathy
Temperance
Temptation
Today
Tolerance
Trouble
Trust
Truth
Unity
Victory
Vision
Worldliness
Worry
Worship
Youth

3. File all poems in a "poem file" under the same subjects used for the sermon titles.

4. File all newspaper clippings, articles, and other illustration material in letter-size folders or envelopes in an "illustration file," using the same subjects.

5. Make a letter-size folder or envelope for each sermon subject chosen for a Sunday during the year.

The length of time involved in cataloguing one's sermonic library in the manner indicated above is between thirty and forty hours for three hundred books of sermons. In most parishes a member with typing ability can be found who, as a labor of love and a service to the church, will care for the typing of the titles without remuneration. A church secretary can readily do all the stenographic work needed during those periods when the work of the office is light. The minister who has no access to secretarial help will discover rich and unsuspected treasures for preaching the word as he does the work himself. In a few months a minister will have saved more time than he expended in creating a usable filing system.

SPECIMEN COMMITTEE REPORTS

The Christian Year in Preaching and Worship, pages 132-37
Midweek Services of Prayer, Bible Study, and Fellowship, pages 137-39
Radio Committee, page 151

CHAPTER 4

How to Provide Worship for All the Church

BASIC PRINCIPLES

1. The supreme purposes of worship, whether public or private, are to glorify God and to commune with him.
2. The church year with its seasons and special days provides the best pattern for richness and variety in worship and music.
3. The service of Holy Communion offers one of the chief opportunities for corporate worship.
4. Worthy religious music greatly enhances the value of any church service.
5. All the worship services of the church and of its organizations deserve the most careful planning and preparation under the guidance of the minister and the committee on worship.
6. Private worship through personal meditation, Bible reading, family worship, and daily prayer pays handsome dividends in successful, Christlike living.

THE new concept of church worship makes it a thrilling, exciting, adventurous experience of the divine presence. Far from being a dull routine, stereotyped repetition of too-familiar phrases of an ancient ritual, it becomes a challenging discovery of the current will of God. Horizons are broadened, personalities are purified, souls become sensitive, and Christians see the vision splendid through the eyes of their heavenly Father.

To realize the divine purposes of corporate and private worship one must take into account the highest and noblest capacities of the total personality. In worship at its best the self is unified and oriented, and all its powers are heightened and tuned to concert pitch. Far from losing identity in a mystic, hazy unconsciousness, all one's faculties become brilliantly aware of the eternal truth, goodness, and beauty which come to one in his communion with his divine Friend. Great Christians have expressed the purposes of worship in these words:

To meet and know God
To have fellowship with God through faith in Jesus Christ
To discover the will of God
To express gratitude and thanksgiving
To receive the grace of God through the sacraments
To feel the presence and peace of the living Christ
To witness to my faith through the creed
To receive the Word of God through Scripture
To join with fellow Christians in praise and prayer
To receive instruction and inspiration
To dedicate and to rededicate my life to God
To find my real self in the presence of God
To see life through the eyes of the Eternal

Outline the Christian year in worship. The Christian calendar offers for worship and music, as it does for preaching, the best possible spiritual framework about which to plan the public services and private devotions through the changing seasons. Growing out of the religious needs of Christians and confirmed in their personal religious experience, the holy days, the sacred seasons, and the memorable dates provide varied emphases that vastly enrich the Christian life of both the church and the believer.

Observing the Christian year in worship has proved extremely helpful to churches of all types and sizes whether they use elaborate liturgy, a modified ritual, or a simple order of service. The days and seasons as they are generally observed by leading American communions, with the exception of saints' days, will be found in the following list. They include most of the important emphases of both historic and contemporary Christianity.

Labor Sunday	Race Relations Sunday
Christian Education Sunday	Ash Wednesday
Rally Day	Lent
World Communion Sunday	Passion Sunday
World Order Sunday	Palm Sunday
Reformation Sunday	Holy Week
Thanksgiving Sunday	Maundy Thursday
Advent	Good Friday
Universal Bible Sunday	Easter Day
Christmas Sunday	National Family Week
Christmas Eve	Mother's Day
Christmas Day	Ascension Sunday
New Year's Eve	Memorial Sunday
New Year's Sunday	Pentecost Sunday
Epiphany Sunday	Trinity Sunday
The Week of Prayer	Independence Sunday

Exalt worship in public services. The supreme privilege accorded to any minister in his priestly function is that of leading his people to the throne of grace in Christian worship. He does not enter the holy of holies for them. Because of the priesthood of all believers, everyone shares in glorifying God, witnessing to his faith in Christ, confessing his sins, and receiving the pardon and blessing from God. Any minister who regards the worship portion of a public service lightly, who fails properly to prepare his mind and heart for it, who conducts divine service in a careless, offhand, slovenly fashion, fails God and his people and is guilty of sacrilege.

The service of *Holy Communion* is Christian worship at its highest. All too often when the sacrament of the Lord's Supper is announced, the minister faces a congregation that is smaller than usual. His people often remain away because they do not fully understand or sense their high privilege and duty. Therefore explain the meaning and purpose of Holy Communion. Indicate the word of the Master, "Do this in remembrance of me." Point out the blessings that come during Communion. Stress the fact that it is the duty of every Christian to receive the sacrament. Hold up the service of Holy Communion as a service of obligation. Encourage families to take Communion together. Thousands of Presbyterian churches, as well as many others, have found that a Communion card delivered or mailed to the home of each member the week before Communion Sunday results in a steadily growing attendance.

Prayer, which is communion with God, is at the very heart of Christian faith and experience. Whether spoken or read, uttered or unexpressed, the prayers of the centuries and the prayers that grow out of the needs of the present have a worthy place. Some "stated prayers" are classic in their aspiration and beauty and, when used wisely, enhance the experience of worship. On the other hand, to recite the Lord's Prayer instead of praying it, to race through it as if trying to set an all-time record, and to fail to drop one's voice so that each worshiper in the congregation may pray that prayer is to rob a congregation of one of the notable climaxes of the service.

The *scripture lesson* is the Word which God has for each worshiper. A psalm, a selection from the Old Testament, a passage from the New Testament, a lesson more or less closely related to the sermon can all be read so as to be a revelation of the presence and will of God.

Flowers, artistically arranged by the altar guild or flower committee, enhance any worship center with loveliness and meaning. Encourage the gift of altar flowers, either as memorials to departed loved ones or as gifts to beautify the house of God. A colored, framed poster listing the dates with the names of the donors of the flowers during the year is procurable at any denominational publishing house. Unusual decorations at appropriate seasons such as Thanksgiving, Christmas, Palm Sunday, Easter, and Children's Day will be gladly undertaken and splendidly arranged by classes or groups invited to take this responsibility.

Counsel with worship leaders of organizations throughout the church. Because worship is becoming an increasingly important part of the activity of most church organizations, ministers are finding it both desirable and necessary to call together the devotional leaders of all church groups for counsel and training. In this church-wide conference stress the high importance of reverence in worship. Discuss the purposes and aims which a service seeks to achieve. Consider the material available for such devotions and suggest ways in which it can be effectively used. Share experiences and invite suggestions for the enrichment of group worship. Encourage each chairman to improve his leadership by more careful preparation and by long-range planning.

Fortunately the "opening exercises" of the dark ages of religious education have given way to graded Christian worship among all church-school and youth groups. Avoiding competition with the regular church service, t church-school literature now offers admirable material for use in worship that is adapted to all ages. Church-school departments in both the children's and youth divisions have by the hundreds built worship centers for their assembly rooms. Whether it is elaborate, with a cross, a Bible, a globe of the world, flowers, and rich, colorful hangings for a background, or simply arranged with but a table on which rest the Bible and offering plates, those departments which have created an altar or worship center have found a new reverence and a deeper sense of the presence of God.

Enlarge the work of the music committee in order that Christian music may make its full contribution to the life of the church. Most music committees mistakenly believe that their duty is done when they have provided an anthem and offertory music for the morning and evening services. Their time, attention, and budget are all too frequently restricted to organ music, the adult choir, the soloists, and the director.

Music committees in recent years have come to sense their clear duty to plan for *all the music of the church* instead of only a portion of it. Among the areas and responsibilities that clearly belong to the church music committee are the following:

1. To consider and study the total musical program of the church
2. To select and to supervise the director, organist, soloist, and chorus choir in close co-operation with the minister
3. To counsel with the various departmental superintendents of the church school for the enrichment of their musical activities
   To encourage the formation of a junior choir and a youth

choir for the church and church school, in co-operation with the board of education

5. To suggest the study and memorization of one great hymn each month by the primary, junior, and intermediate departments of the church school

6. To assume responsibility for the care of church hymnals and choir robes

7. To co-operate with the director of music in the discovery and enlistment of musical talent in the congregation

8. To present the itemized musical budget for the coming year to the finance committee, covering the musical needs of the entire church

Churches should strive to assure better choral and organ music for their services. Protestant Christians are rapidly realizing that the oratorios, anthems, solos, and hymns that have arisen out of a deep, warmhearted, personal religious experience of Protestants are far richer than those produced by any other division of the universal Christian church. Because of this rich musical heritage, it is unpardonable for any church to present music that is repetitious, monotonous, inferior, or inappropriate. The public schools, colleges and universities, and radio-television networks in many of their programs have vastly improved musical taste and lifted the level of musical appreciation.

The competent director chooses the anthems and other special numbers several months ahead. He determines his choice by what will be appropriate to the season, the Sunday, and the sermon theme for the day. The discerning minister selects hymns suitable to the spirit of the service and the theme of the sermon, avoiding, with some notable exceptions, the repetition of any hymn during the church year. Together they encourage improved congregational singing, and arrange for an exchange of anthems with neighboring churches or secure the loan of new anthems from libraries of religious music.

Cultivate family worship in order that the family may share in the Christian development of each of its members. Perhaps the most strategic emphasis of recent Christian education has been that placed on the Christian home as a chief factor in personal, Christlike development. The modern family does all too few things together, with the result that its members are only loosely held together by need and convenience. Christian homes not only have proved that "families that pray together stay together" but also have provided those ties of the spirit that give security, strength, and meaning to personal life.

Churches of all communions provide guidance in the establishing of a family altar and help in developing family worship. They provide graces for all ages to be said by successive members of the family. They encourage Bible reading and religious conversations on those occasions when all members of the home are together. Parents find scores of prayers are available for themselves and for their children, with devotional helps that express aspiration and answer personal needs.

The minister should commend personal, daily devotions by every member of the church. It is sound psychology as well as sound religion to begin, continue, and end the day with God. Bishop Ralph S. Cushman has caught the spirit expressed by the experience of millions in the words of his poem "The Secret."

> I met God in the morning
>   When my day was at its best,
> And His Presence came like sunrise,
>   Like a glory in my breast.

All day long the Presence lingered,
    All day long He stayed with me,
And we sailed in perfect calmness
    O'er a very troubled sea.

Other ships were blown and battered,
    Other ships were sore distressed,
But the winds that seemed to drive them
    Brought to us a peace and rest.

Then I thought of other mornings,
    With a keen remorse of mind,
When I too had loosed the moorings,
    With the Presence left behind.

So I think I know the secret,
    Learned from many a troubled way:
You must seek Him in the morning
    If you want Him through the day! [1]

Millions of Christians start the day with private devotions based on a monthly or quarterly devotional booklet such as *Today* or *The Upper Room.* In the scripture lesson, the thought for the day, and the prayer they find the faith, courage, and strength that they require to live victoriously. Churches everywhere remember the aged and shut-in of the congregation by sending or delivering these devotional booklets regularly to them.

Church members join with their minister at his request, "sometime between seven o'clock and nine o'clock in the morning," in united meditation and prayer. Each senses the presence of the heavenly Father, and practices that

[1] From *Spiritual Hilltops,* copyright 1932 by Ralph S. Cushman. By permission of Abingdon-Cokesbury Press.

presence during the day. Each finds his powers heightened, and feels his mind and soul strengthened; he comes to the end of the day with the peace and grace of God in his heart. In the evening, as "the shadows lengthen and the evening comes, and the busy world is hushed," the Christian knows that "something out of this world" has come into his experience through the day.

A wise Quaker caught the spirit of Christian worship when he said, "The end of the service is the beginning of service." After Christians have met God in church and home, they go out divinely commissioned to live the Christlike life and to help Christ transform the world.

SPECIMEN COMMITTEE REPORTS

CHAPTER 5

How to Improve Your Church School

BASIC PRINCIPLES

1. The church school is the most important organization in the church for Christian education and character building.
2. Planning on a long-range basis is indispensable to any growing program of Christian education.
3. Improved teaching and an enriched curriculum must precede any permanent increase in attendance and membership.
4. An intelligently planned program will pay handsome dividends in Christian loyalty and church membership.
5. The primary aim of the church school is to help growing personalities of all ages to become progressively Christlike in spirit, thought, and conduct.

THE most interesting Christian educational meeting of the year comes in May, when our board of education meets with the teachers and officers of our church school to plan their work for the coming year," said the pastor of a large and growing church in the Middle West. "Everyone present expresses his opinions freely, whether they are complimentary or critical. Each offers his suggestions for strengthening and expanding the activities of the church school. It is a splendid example of co-operative planning and creative discussion. Because we plan, we make progress year after year."

In contrast to this intelligent, statesmanlike approach to Christian education is the careless, hit-and-miss, slipshod, extemporaneous improvising that is such a tragic, pitiful substitute for religious training. To ask for volunteer teachers, to select leaders carelessly, to leave a class without a teacher, to fail to follow up absentees, to make no effort to recruit new members, and to fail to provide the best possible religious instruction are bitter sins against children, young people, and adults of the church school.

Discover educational needs and opportunities. Chief among these will be the Sunday morning session of the church school, where graded worship and instruction are provided for all ages. Christian education in the home represents a vital and largely unexplored area for Christian nurture. The Christian activities of youth provide a field for fellowship and service for growing personalities, while adult education offers unlimited prospects for any church in the country's increasing adult population. Devotional booklets and pamphlets on religious themes, Christian drama and forum discussions of civic, moral, and religious themes provide open doors of interest, fellowship, and service.

Who shall be responsible for this long-range planning? Nearly all denominations have in recent years provided for the creation of a board of education in each local church. Composed of representative church members, this board has the responsibility and oversight of the total program of Christian education. Among the key persons on this board are the church-school superintendent, the departmental superintendents of the church school, the president of the youth organization, the chairman of the board of education, the director of Christian education, and the minister. With its power to determine policies, select teachers, choose goals, and initiate new projects, the board of education is the ideal group to determine the broad educational plans of the church for the months ahead.

The board of education can appraise the needs and opportunities of the church school by giving frank, factual answers to such questions as these: *use*

How well has our church school done its task during the past year?

What has been its chief weaknesses and its major strengths?

Has our church-school attendance increased or declined? How much?

How well are we teaching the children and youth of our church and community?

What new equipment do we need in the several departments?

How can we secure better teachers?

How can we provide training for our present teachers?

Do we need a young adult class? A married couples' class? A young people's class?

How can worship be improved?

Should the church-school budget be increased? How much?

Are our records well kept?

Do we follow up our absentees as promptly as we ought?

Are we trying continuously to enlist new members? *How?*

What weekday activities in adult education should we undertake?

Do we encourage the reading of religious publications and devotional literature as much as we ought?

Do we give young people as large a part as they can assume in planning their own program?

Honest answers to these and other questions will reveal to any board of education the areas of greatest interest and most promising achievement.

The educational aims of any church school group themselves in six general divisions, which include many of the following:

1. *Organization:*
   a) The faithful creation of the kind of educational organization recommended by the denomination
   b) A complete set of permanent records
   c) The appointment or election of qualified persons to fill any existing vacancies
   d) The appointment of an assistant superintendent in charge of attendance and membership
   e) The selection of a director of Christian education, either paid or unpaid, from among those who have educational training and experience

2. *Attendance:*
   a) An intensive church-school attendance crusade during September and October
   b) A careful follow-up of absentees through assigning their names to the teacher and members of the class
   c) An attendance goal of 25 per cent larger average attendance than the previous year
   d) The apportionment of a fair share of this attendance increase to each class and department of the church school
   e) A continuous accent on "Every-Sunday Attendance by Every Member of the Church School"

3. *Membership:*
   a) A new-member goal representing an increase of 20 per cent in the total membership of the church school
   b) The apportioning of a reasonable part of this membership increase to each class and department
   c) The appointment of a membership committee in each youth and adult class
   d) A prospect list with names and addresses of prospective members for each class and department, a permanent

master file of these names being kept in the office of the church-school secretary

e) A friendly call on each member of the church who is not a member of the church school, inviting him into a congenial class

f) The recognition and honoring of new members as they join

4. *Teaching:*

a) A card index of all prospective teachers in the congregation, graded according to the departments in which they can best serve

b) The appointment of an associate teacher for each class

c) A teacher training course each year for all teachers

d) The purchase of two or three teacher training books for each department, these to be the beginning of a leadership library

5. *Equipment:*

a) The reconditioning and repainting of the chairs and tables of the several departments

b) The purchase of religious pictures

c) The securing of up-to-date maps of biblical countries

d) A worship center for one or more of the departments

e) The purchase or borrowing of equipment for audio-visual education

f) A three-year program of equipment purchases to bring the physical properties of the church school to the desired level

6. *New Projects:*

a) The formation of a younger married couples' class

b) The "adoption of a native missionary" as a project toward which to devote the church-school missionary offering

c) The taking of a friendly, community-wide census in co-operation with other churches

d) The selection of a project of service, either for the

church or for the community, by each class or department

e) The printing or duplicating of an attractive folder to be used to increase church-school attendance and membership

f) The institution of the expanded session for the children's division of the church school

g) The organization and training of a children's choir

h) The explanation, study, and memorization of one new hymn each month

i) A program for encouraging children and youth to make annual pledges to the church and to use contribution envelopes each Sunday

Plan Christian education on a twelve-month basis. The themes of the monthly board of education and teachers' conference meeting for the whole year should be outlined. In addition to the usual business of the monthly board of education meeting, such as departmental reports, administrative problems, and a preview of the chief emphases and events of the coming month or two, officials and teachers alike find a welcome stimulus in having some qualified person present some Christian educational theme as the outstanding feature of the monthly meeting. Followed by a period of questions and discussion, presentations of such subjects as the following have kindled interest, broadened knowledge, and strengthened church-school morale:

September: A Larger and Better Church School
October: How Is Our Church Organized?
November: Christians Are World Citizens
December: How to Use the Bible Today
January: The Christian Movement Abroad
    (foreign missions)

February: The Christian Movement at Home (home
missions)

March: The Basic Beliefs of a Christian

April: Christian Stewardship

May: Our Plans for the Coming Year (the annual
church-school planning conference)

June: The Moral and Religious Needs of Our Community

July: Religion in the Home

August: Audio-visual Aids

A wealth of other subjects that relate directly and in-
directly to the educational service rendered by the church
school can be used to expand and enrich the Christian
educational program of the church.

All classes and departments of the church school should
observe the special days and seasons of the Christian education year. When viewed across a twelve-month period,
these holy days and religious periods form an impressive
unity:

Return Sunday signals the opening of the intensive
church-school year, coming as it does the Sunday after the
public schools open.

Christian Education Sunday, the fourth Sunday in September, opens Religious Education Week and affords
churches the opportunity to feature Christian education.
All teachers, associate teachers, and officers sit together in
the morning service as guests of honor, with an impressive dedication or consecration ceremony at the close.
This Sunday is often celebrated as "Rally Day."

World Communion Sunday, the first Sunday in October,
keynotes "Every Church-School Member Present," and
"Every Church Member Receiving Communion." This
Sunday marks the opening of the nation-wide Church

Loyalty Crusade, which progressive church schools parallel with a church-school attendance crusade of their own. This Sunday is also observed as Rally Sunday in many churches.

World Order Sunday, the third Sunday in October, emphasizes the fact that all Christians are members of the Christian world brotherhood.

Thanksgiving Sunday is a day when, through departmental decorations, worship services, and an offering for others, church-school members can express their gratitude to God.

The Christmas season and Christmas Sunday express the Christmas spirit through "White Gifts for the King," drama, songs, and stories.

New Year's Sunday affords the opportunity for dedication toward improved aims and more Christlike lives.

Membership Sunday in the church school climaxes with a personal commitment the long period of preparation during which the pupil has learned of Christ and his church.

Lent, the forty days, not including Sundays, preceding Easter, offers a priceless period for self-examination, self-sacrifice, increased Christlikeness.

Palm Sunday symbolizes the triumph of the Son of God, who at last shall win all the kingdoms of the world to himself.

Good Friday enables all Christians to enter into the fellowship of Christ's suffering for the redemption of the world.

Easter Day renews assurance of everlasting life as it brings immortality to light.

Mother's Day, the festival of the Christian home, focuses attention on the Christianization of family relationships.

Children's Day again exalts the priceless opportunity of molding young life according to Christian patterns.

Student Day holds up the values of college education in preparation for life.

These occasions, with others that feature the Christian year, offer energetic and resourceful leaders a superb background for Christian educational projects.

Interest parents in the church school. One of the most promising trends in Christian education is to be found in the growing partnership of parents and teachers, of home and church school, in the service of growing Christian personalities. The new church-school curriculum of the Presbyterian Church, U.S.A., has wisely accented and provided for the sharing of educational tasks by Christian parents in their home to a far greater degree than in most other communions.

A "Parents' Day" in each department will acquaint the fathers and mothers with the activities of worship and study. Call together the parents of children for a discussion of the moral and religious problems that face them. Invite criticisms and suggestions for improvement in the church-school program. Provide parents with graces and prayers, graded to the age levels of their children. Encourage parents to subscribe to one of the church-school magazines that discuss the role of the Christian home in the steady development of personality. Provide for a parents' class at the church-school hour in order that they may share in the Christian educational process. These definite projects, which enable parents to share in the privilege and responsibility of the religious development of their children, will effectively undergird any adequate program of Christian education.

Increase church-school attendance. "We increased the

average attendance of our church school one third over the previous September and October by the simple device of stressing every-Sunday attendance and following up all absentees," said an alert minister who gives eight or ten hours of his busy time each week to the church school. Some churches on the Tuesday after Labor Day mail to every member of their church school a postal card announcing Return Sunday, and urging every pupil and every teacher to be in his place that day. The Tuesday after Return Sunday another persuasive card is mailed to all church-school members who were absent on Return Sunday, a technique that increases attendance by 10 or 15 per cent.

Hundreds of church schools are following up the success of Rally Day by writing a letter early in the week to every teacher, enclosing a list of the names, addresses, and the telephone numbers of his class members who have not yet returned. This letter is typed in triplicate, the other two copies being mailed on October 15 and October 30, with the lines drawn through the names of all absentees who have returned to date. This has the advantage of fixing the teacher's attention on those absentees who require a personal call or a telephone inquiry to bring them back to class.

Some churches use a system of attendance awards, as do the Boy Scouts and the Rotary Club. Others encourage a friendly rivalry among classes of approximately the same size. Still others graphically present the attendance goal in terms of a chart for each class or department, that the ideal and obligation of each church-school group may be visualized and attained. Any church school anywhere can substantially increase the number it serves in the name of Christ by intelligent planning and hard work.

Enlarge church-school membership by inviting non-members into the fellowship and study of the school. A rich source of recruits is to be found in the membership of the church itself, where records reveal that about one half of the members of the average church are not related to the church school. Especially easy to win are the new members of the church immediately after they are received, as they are then most eager for Christian fellowship.

The friends of church-school members often require only a friendly invitation to bring them both to the class sessions and to the social affairs of the class of their choice. To present them to the class; to introduce them to new friends; to bring them to class social affairs; and to relate them to some service activity of the class is to win them to regular attendance and permanent class membership.

The religious illiteracy among the hundreds of children, young people, and adults in most communities should challenge and arouse sincere Christians from their indifference and lethargy. They have immortal tidings in their mortal hands. They represent the abundant life for everyone. The Saviour of men would have the church school serve them.

Publicity has been used by evil men to popularize habits that are harmful and ideas that are evil, but it can be used also by Christian people in the church school in making attractive Christian fellowship and the Christlike life. Carry some announcements or news concerning the church school and its growing work in every issue of the weekly bulletin. Print or duplicate an attractive folder which lists the departments, classes, and teachers of the entire church school. Duplicate a four-page folder—it often is called "Church School News"—which will include short articles of interest about new teachers, service projects,

religious music and drama, and events and movements
that will increase the interest of the members of both the
church school and the church.

Many local newspapers will gladly print news articles
about the church-school annual election, the names of
those promoted from one department to another, the
officers elected annually by any class, social affairs, with
the names of the members of the committee in charge, and
the purchase of new equipment, as well as any unusual
events or outstanding achievement.

Using the remembered experience of the past as the
foundation, and fitting the building stones of new plans and
projects chosen for each coming year, any church school
can improve and expand its program of Christian service
as well as enjoy a steady growth in attendance and membership.

SPECIMEN COMMITTEE REPORTS

CHAPTER 6

How to Encourage Youth to Plan Ahead

BASIC PRINCIPLES
   1. A well-balanced youth program, unfolding through the year, is a powerful force for strengthening the interest and loyalty of young people.
   2. Youth must always play a major role in the planning of their own activities.
   3. Plans and projects must feature the Christian answer to the needs and interests of young people.
   4. A vital, colorful schedule of Christian worship, friendship, and service will always challenge and win a ready response from youth.
   5. Skillful guidance by able lay counselors is essential to the progress and success of any worth-while youth movement.

THE youth activities of a church of about five hundred members were revolutionized by the coming of a new minister. Strangely enough, he had retired from the pastorate because of age, and was serving the church only until a successor was called. He found the Sunday evening youth group numbered four or five, who were discouraged and hopeless over the prospect.

He invited these faithful few, with several other young people of the parish, to his home for an evening of fellowship and planning. He encouraged them to speak frankly of their lack of success, to tell of their chief interests and wishes, and to pool their opinions concerning what a strong

65

Christian youth group should do. They reorganized their group around areas of interest which they themselves selected. With the added leadership of a young doctor and his wife, whom they helped choose as their counselors, their numbers grew to an average attendance of thirty-five. The resources of interest and leadership were present in that church all the time; they needed only to be discovered and used.

Discover what youth need and want. An outspoken older boy in his senior year in high school belligerently said: "We're not children any longer. We're growing up. We don't want the church to do everything for us. Older people don't understand us, and sometimes we don't understand ourselves. But we know some of the things we need, and we want a part in planning these." Among the important interests and needs of young people are the following, arranged in five groups and cast for vividness in the first person:

Personality needs: "I want to do something worth while and win approval. I want to count for something and amount to something. I like to lead. I want to win."

Home relationships: "I like my mother and dad; they are good eggs. They are rather old-fashioned in most ways, but they mean all right. Friction and trouble sometimes break out, and I think how good it will be when I can get out on my own. I wish we could get along better than we do."

Mental growth: "School is all right, but I sometimes wonder what good it does to study. With television, radio, and the movies a fellow learns a lot. I suppose an education has value, and I know I have to get good grades if I am to get anywhere. How can I find new interests? How can I find out what I want to do? How can I decide between two or three things that look good as a vocation?"

Social interests: "I like friends and parties. It's fun to date the decent fellows, unless they get too sentimental or serious. I want to know how I can judge the comrades and companions I should choose. I want to know how to meet the social pressures and how to keep my Christian ideals. I want to be popular without being cheap. Sometime I hope to fall in love with the right one, and I only want to know how to tell the imitation from the real thing. I want my church to be the center of my social life. It's better to have clean fun in a church than in a night club."

Religious needs: "We young people are naturally religious. I believe in God and heaven. I want to know how religion can help me with my everyday life. Who is Christ? Who am I? What should I pray for? What about the church? Why don't the churches all get together? What is right and what is wrong? How can I really know God cares for me?"

Organize a youth council of leading young people, that the youth of the church may do the major part of their own planning. These elected representatives ought to come from the top 10 per cent of the youth group members in ability, standing, resourcefulness, and leadership. In a small church the number need not be more than three, while in a large church the number may be seven or nine, representing the several groups of young people. They will elect their own council officers, with the minister and the counselors as ex officio members. Meetings may be held each month to review the events and activities of the past month, as well as to plan those for the period ahead. As a clearinghouse for ideas and plans, as a training camp for young leadership, as a safety valve for friction and "gripes," and as a board of strategy to give definiteness and direction to youth energies, the youth council is unsurpassed as a technique and tool for successful youth work.

The best possible youth counselors should be selected in order that the youth group may have the advantage of wiser guidance and more mature judgment. While young people should never be forced to accept a counselor they do not wish, they should be guided so that they may select one of the best-qualified couples in the congregation as their adult leaders. Usually from the young adult group, this couple should be socially acceptable, young in outlook, mentally alert, well educated, loyal to Christian ideals, and faithful to the church. Often the selection is made from among the parents of young people, those who know youth problems and have a personal interest in the group.

These counselors, as a part of their duty, will meet with the young people for their devotional service and fellowship hour each Sunday evening, will share their social life and play, will counsel them in their preparation for leadership in devotional meetings and discussion periods, will guide them in the planning of their social affairs, will be father- and mother-confessors to them in their perplexing problems, and will always represent Christ and his church. In addition to relieving the minister of the many details of the youth organization, they will often perform these duties in a far more acceptable fashion than he can. A strong representative youth council, guided by able, interested counselors, assures an active, growing youth fellowship in any church.

Define aims to interest and help youth. Youth counselors, young people, teachers of youth, and ministers have given the following answers when asked to state the chief purposes and major objectives of their youth groups:

To help young people to grow in their Christian life and
    experience
To aid them in finding for themselves the best in life
To help them as growing persons
To perpare them for their chosen places in life
To help them solve their problems
To provide a congenial group of friends for them
To hold young people steady in difficult days
To serve youth in the name of Christ
To provide religious guidance for young people
To lead young people to Christ
To teach youth how to live the Christlike life
To help them understand what life is all about
To help them to become better Christians

With such aims in mind the members of the youth council can co-operatively choose the chief features of a strong
program for the year. The finest possible materials and
suggestions available are those recommended by the youth
division of one's own denomination. This outline of
themes and activities, when prepared by experts familiar
with the most successful Christian youth projects and plans
of all communions in the United States, should be the
foundation and framework for any local youth group.
These should never be slavishly followed by the youth
council but will be carefully considered and wisely adapted
to local needs. With these plans before them, youth councils have asked questions like the following in these five
chief areas of youth interest and activity:

1. *The Sunday evening service of worship and discussion:* How can our services of worship be made more helpful? Do we need a worship center? How can we improve
our music? How can we get more members to take part?
What guest speakers can be secured? How can the themes

be prepared to make them more interesting and helpful? What subjects of local interest might be included? Would more discussion of the subject by the group prove interesting? How can we increase the spirit of reverence?

2. *Membership and attendance:* What is our present membership and average attendance? How many young people should we have in our membership? What goals ought we to set in membership and attendance? Should we have a campaign to enlist new members? How can we persuade other young people to join us? Who among our friends could we personally invite to join? How can we work them into the life of our group so that they will remain permanently with us?

3. *Social life and parties:* How often should we get together for an evening of fellowship and fun? Is once a month too often? Could we make a schedule of parties, setting the dates and places for the months ahead? Might some of these be held at the church and others at our homes? How can we enrich the social fellowship of our Sunday evening hour? Could we divide our membership into groups of four, making them responsible for the program and refreshments for our parties? How can we take part more than we do in the church-wide suppers and social evenings of our church?

4. *Community and world friendship:* How can we make our discussion of Christian missions more interesting? Should we "adopt" some Christian young person in a foreign country and contribute to his schooling and support? What should we know about the United Nations and its international work? What is the Christian solution to the race problem? In what areas and movements in our own community should we share?

5. *Christian service:* What could we do for our own

church? Could we build a bulletin board, care for the church lawn, paint or varnish the church-school chairs or serve at dinners and banquets? Could we form a youth quartet or choir? Could we help organize a Boy Scout or Girl Scout group? Might we be responsible for flowers on the altar or communion table each Sunday during the summer? How can we throw our Christian influence into the solution of youth and community problems?

Counsel youth in carrying out their program, especially in areas which are most basic to successful work with young people in the church.

The *Sunday evening service of worship and discussion* is the heart of any vital youth program in any local church. Its high importance cannot be overestimated. If the order of service is careless and unplanned, if its spirit is one of flippancy or irreverence, if the theme of the evening is poorly presented, and if discussion is nonexistent, then the service will fail at its most crucial point. But if the features of the service have been carefully chosen, if appropriate hymns have been selected and good special music provided, if the subject for discussion shows evidence of careful preparation and clear thinking, and if creative comment is offered by the young people at its close, the evening will be both popular and constructive.

Amazing improvement in the quality and variety of resource material for youth services has taken place in all communions. When one surveys the carefully planned units and series on such themes as God, Christ, the church, service, peace, missions, race, prayer, brotherhood, youth problems, and Bible study in both the Old and the New Testament, one is convinced that there is no excuse for repetition or lack of interest. Increasing numbers of counselors and pastors are adopting a splendid technique of spending an hour with each young person in planning the worship features, in outlining the subject, and in framing questions for general discussion.

Social life is of the utmost importance to young people, and they should be encouraged to make the church the center of the youth social events of the community. Friendship and sociability can be powerful magnets to draw young people into the Christian circle. Carefully plan every party so that there is not a dull moment during the evening. Invite prospective members to these youth-fun nights. Make sure that they meet all the members of the youth group. Make the newcomer and the timid person feel at home. Cordially invite strangers to come the following Sunday to church, to church school, and to the Sunday evening fellowship.

Membership and attendance of the youth groups can be increased by supplementing the continuous recruiting efforts with two special campaigns. One of these will naturally begin in the early autumn—opening on Rally Day if the day is being observed at this season. Prepare a folder covering the next three months' program of meetings, leaders, subjects, and social affairs. Accent one hundred per cent attendance at all youth gatherings. Use the printed or duplicated folder in the effort to interest friends. Give them a "sales talk" on what the program and organization mean to you. Offer to call for them for the next meeting or party. Climax this autumn effort on a Sunday about four weeks later.

The ideal time for a second movement is either at the beginning of the new year or the opening of Lent. Both seasons lend themselves admirably to the important task of bringing young people into the Christian fellowship.

Guide youth in sharing in the church's work. Up-to-date churches no longer are asking, "What can we do for our young people that we may hold them in our church?" Rather are they asking, "How can we challenge and guide our young people in such a way that they will eagerly desire to give their time and talents to Christian service?"

The frequent failure of churches and ministers to include their young people in all the church-wide movements of the Christian year is a grievous sin of omission. The absence of this important segment of the church, which will constitute the church of tomorrow, is unpardonable shortsightedness and bad strategy. Important movements, events, and crusades—such as evangelism, church loyalty, pledging, special offerings, and church-wide planning—should have their proper contingent of young people. With fine wisdom the Presbyterian Church, U.S.A., encourages its young people to prepare and raise their youth budget as a project in financial churchmanship. The Methodist Church on the national level has provided for youth representatives on practically all of its general boards and commissions, while individual churches often appoint a youth or a young adult to membership on all important committees.

Young people will more willingly and eagerly enlist for full-time Christian service as ministers, missionaries, or directors of Christian education if they have had the privilege and the joy of sharing in the work of their local church.

SPECIMEN COMMITTEE REPORT
Youth Activities, pages 142-43

CHAPTER 7

How to Develop Lay Leadership

BASIC PRINCIPLES

1. The priesthood of believers gives laymen a divine right to share in the leadership of the church.
2. Ample talent for all the tasks of the church can be found or developed in any congregation.
3. The minister by training and experience is the "leader of leaders" in any congregation.
4. The "leadership load" should be spread as widely as possible among the members of the church.
5. A "job analysis" and a "personnel analysis" are indispensable in selecting the ablest leader for any position.
6. The minister should shift all the administrative work possible to the laymen, in so far as they have or can develop the ability to carry it.
7. An associate or assistant leader should be chosen for every lay position in the church.
8. The real strength of a church is largely determined by the caliber and ability of its lay leadership.

THE minister and laymen of every church will do well to remember that Jesus chose twelve laymen as his disciples. He called them from their tasks in the workaday world that they might proclaim and create with him the kingdom of God on earth. He displayed the highest strategy in training and commissioning laymen as leaders in the church.

The chief problem in any church is its leadership, ministerial and lay. Three Ohio churches, within a stone's throw of one another, are typical of the wise and the foolish kingdom builders. In one the minister tries to do every-thing—a sort of one-man army of the Lord. He ignores the official church committees and usurps their powers—"be-cause it's easier to do it myself." He works hard but not intelligently. In a neighboring church the pastor boasts of "leaving everything to my laymen." He is a master in the art of giving his church school, his youth group, and his official committees absent treatment. He is the occupant of a pulpit rather than the minister of a Christian church. Neither of these churches is growing in numbers or in vital strength.

The third church is outstanding in the community be-cause of its excellent preaching, its superior church school, its growing groups, and its broad service at home and abroad. The open secret of its help and growing influence is to be found in the close partnership of pastor and people. They share as they co-operatively plan the work of their church. This minister spends four or five hours each week advising and inspiring his lay leaders. He makes it a cardi-nal principle of his ministry to do no administrative work for which he can find or train a competent layman. Be-cause his laymen carry the administrative load, he finds ample time for sermon preparation, reading, community activities, and those pastoral functions which he alone can perform.

The priesthood of all believers gives every Christian the divine right and duty to share in the work of the local church. The inexhaustible skills and talents of the mem-bers of any congregation represent its richest unused assets.

The good minister of Jesus Christ will always regard himself as "a leader of leaders." His role is not that of a dictator or swivel-chair director who operates by remote control. He will neither do everything himself nor neglect any phase of the varied work of his church. He will be the faithful guide, the wise counselor, the trusted instructor, the director of personnel, the builder of morale, and the chief servant of the servants of the Lord.

Choose an able nominating committee to co-operate with the minister in the important task of selecting, training, and developing the best lay leaders. The minister must never monopolize this strategic task but rather must give it his most conscientious thought and statesmanlike guidance. Naturally he will play a leading role in the leadership drama because he knows the general program of the church, is acquainted with leadership needs, is familiar with the capacities and backgrounds of the members of the church, and often can more easily persuade them to assume important responsibilities than can anyone else in the church.

So far as local and denominational practice permit, a single nominating committee should name the nominees for all the congregation-wide offices and committees of the church, and should serve throughout the year. The committee must take time to assemble information about the talents of all members of the church and then, with the pastor, pool their opinions and judgments about the gifts of each person and the area of service in which he is best qualified. Such study is indispensable to finding a task for everyone and everyone for a task. It is also in line with the best practice followed in personnel offices of successful business concerns. Without it the committee is likely to be reduced to calling for volunteers, which is one of the worst possible methods, because it bases leadership selection on impulse or chance.

In preparing the annual list of committee chairmen and

members, the nominating committee will ask, among others, the following questions:

Are the official positions of the church concentrated in the hands of too few members or are they widely distributed?

Do a few laymen dominate the committees and life of the church?

Are the officials older or younger than the average for our community?

What percentage of the officials are in their thirties, forties, fifties, sixties, and seventies?

What new or younger men and women should be added to the officiary and its committees?

What positions are now unfilled?

What new committees or positions should be created?

What are the qualities of character and personality needed for the several official positions?

Could not many of the committees be enlarged to include new and younger members?

Should not an assistant or an associate be appointed as vice-chairman of each committee, to serve in case of the illness, removal, or death of the chairman?

The nominating committee should plan to *spread the work load* among a large number of lay men and women. Any congregation that is dominated by one or two laymen labors under a severe and dangerous handicap. Wise and benevolent though any leader may be, he is apt to throttle the honest opinions and stultify the judgment of others. All too many "wait to see what Brother Smith will think about this matter." When through age he becomes ultra-conservative or querulous, he retards the progress of the church. When he passes on, there are few if any strong leaders to take his place.

Make an analysis of the number of positions and committee memberships which each official holds. It may prove startling to discover that one man holds three or four chairmanships, with positions on several other important committees. Such a condition is never the result of intelligent, thoughtful planning but results from drifting along the line of least resistance.

To say that a church is "overorganized" is to utter a thoughtless cliché for which there is usually no truth or foundation in fact. These churches are rather "underorganized," or "badly organized," or "incompetently led."

Each local church will be wise to follow in so far as possible the organizational plan recommended by the denomination to which it belongs. The large church will add to the list of standing boards and committees a number of special ones to care for its new or special projects. The smaller congregation will appoint only those committees that are suited to its basic needs, such as worship and music, education, membership and evangelism, missions and community service, and finance.

The nominating committee should also plan to *lower the average age* of the church's leadership. Churches as well as aging individuals sometimes suffer from hardening of the arteries. Unless the youth of the church is renewed by the frequent infusion of new life, the leadership of any church runs a grave risk of becoming aged and ultraconservative.

Make an age-group study of the officials of the church. Compare this with the percentage of these same age groups in the population of the community. Decide how many younger church members should be appointed to bring the official age group in line with the community norm. Outline a five-year program for lowering the average age of the church board. During the first year, if the age average of the board is fifty-five, nominate three or four who are in the forty-five to fifty-five age group, in order that the possible friction between young and old may be reduced to a minimum. The second year nominate four or five between the ages of forty and forty-five. During the remaining three years select nominees who are in their thirties or late twenties. This gradual process can be strengthened by the appointment of younger men and women to the official committees of the church. Across a five-year period one church reduced its average official age from fifty-four years to forty-five years without friction or criticism of any kind.

It is important to *provide able associates* or assistants for all positions of leadership in the church. No university football team would do without the second and third teams of its football squad, nor would any department of an automobile factory fail to choose an assistant foreman. Surely God's work through the Christian church deserves an equally sound and efficient organization. The associate chairman, carefully chosen by the nominating committee, acts as chairman in case of the illness or absence of the chairman. He studies and becomes familiar with the purposes, program, and leadership needs of the committee. To him the committee can delegate responsibility for certain parts of its work. He is able and usually willing to step into the chairmanship in case a change in leadership is indicated.

The nominating committee can *co-operate with classes and other organizations* in the choice of their leaders by sharing information about the talents of members and by taking such offices into account in their own planning. The minister himself should grasp every opportunity to counsel with the nominating committees of these groups. Every minister has witnessed the rise and fall, the ebb and flow, of the life of one or more organizations in his church. The vitality, value, and outreach of a class or group will be determined largely by the officers elected to guide it under the leadership of its president. The conscientious minister will find this one of his most delicate and difficult tasks, for he must, if possible, avoid "taking sides" or "playing favorites." It becomes his duty, however, to give counsel and help to those organizations needing assistance in order that they may have an aggressive, gifted leader, a well-rounded organization of suitable officers, and a broad worth-while program of Christian service.

Analyze positions and personnel available to fill them. To find "the right man for the right task" alert churches are taking a chapter out of the book of modern business. The personnel office of a great commercial concern is a fascinating place. On individual cards one finds all the pertinent information concerning each employee or prospective employee, such as age, family, interests, education, positions held, temperament, and ability. With a "job analysis" of the skills required for an unfilled position before him, the personnel manager can with reasonable assurance select from four or five possible candidates the one most likely to succeed.

While no such elaborate system of records can be kept in most churches, any church can build up a talent file of information about its members that will be invaluable to the nominating committee, the church school superintendent, and leaders of committees and organizations, as well as the pastor. A Christian survey of the membership will uncover a wealth of lay talent. Hundreds of churches have been astounded at the variety and richness of the abilities of their members, as revealed by a talent-interest questionnaire mailed to each member of the church. After such a survey of the current membership a copy of the questionnaire should be sent to each new member received into the church, that he may be more firmly built into its fellowship. A sample of such a questionnaire, in card form for easy filing, is shown on page 82.

As for the "job analysis," any nominating committee and minister can list the personal qualities needed for any position by asking such questions as these: Does this job need a younger or an older person? Does it require unusual balance and judgment? Should the person chosen be outstanding in the congregation or would someone less well known suitable? Does the task require a high degree of executive ability?

Select competent leaders. To choose the most qualified member for a given chairmanship ask these questions: What three members most fully possess the qualities needed for this position? Which of the three does not now have a prominent position or chairmanship? Is he able to get his fellow members to work at the assigned task, or is he inclined to do everything himself? Does he follow through? Does he possess ability enough to discharge this task successfully?

Because any layman may be entirely competent in one position but quite unfit for another, the nominating committee must frankly, freely, and in all confidence express its Christian judgment in selecting leaders for Christ's church. Among the general qualities in a layman that make for strong and effective leadership are the following: power to think clearly, persistence in a good cause, willingness to accept and discharge responsibility, loyalty to and love of the church, and skill in getting others to work with him. In addition he needs specific qualities of ability and ex-

Name _____

Address _____

Telephone _____

MY STEWARDSHIP OF MY TIME, TALENTS, AND SERVICE

I SHALL BE GLAD TO SERVE, AS REQUESTED, IN THE FOLLOWING WAYS:

☐ Calling on prospective members

☐ Visiting the sick or shut-ins

☐ Teaching in the church school

☐ Leading a youth group as counselor

☐ Singing in the chorus choir

☐ Working with Girl Scouts or Boy Scouts

☐ Helping in the women's organizations

☐ Supervising recreation

☐ Helping in the church office

☐ Sharing in dramatics

☐ Playing the piano

☐ Assisting with church suppers

☐ Serving as a committee member

☐ Ushering

SERVING IN OTHER WAYS:

perience in line with the position for which he is considered. A successful businessman or banker knows finances. A successful salesman can serve effectively as the chairman of the membership and evangelism committee, while a newspaperman is acquainted with publicity. A public school teacher, with personality, knows the educational methods needed in the church school, while a gifted couple in their forties, who rank in the upper 20 per cent of the membership of the church in loyalty, culture, and intelligence, can often give remarkable leadership to a young adult group.

Stimulate officers to work. To persuade a chosen individidual to accept a given assignment and carry it out with enthusiasm is largely a matter of kingdom salesmanship. The prospective leader must know that he has been chosen from the entire membership of the church for this specific task. The project or office should be presented to him as a great opportunity to serve Christ and the church. Interest must be kindled by describing the opportunity for service, and assurance given of the complete confidence of the nominating committee in his ability and willingness to serve. He will be complimented to know the valid reasons that led to his selection. He must not be permitted to say No except for extremely valid reasons. If he remains reluctant, he should be challenged to give the task the best he has for a period of one, two, or three months before he makes his final decision. Nine out of ten qualified individuals can be persuaded to accept if they have been intelligently chosen and competently interviewed.

It is important to *help each leader see his complete task* in terms of the coming twelve months. The recruit needs a picture of his entire responsibility. Most church activities naturally group themselves in a given area according to the four seasons of the year, autumn, winter, spring, and summer. The competent minister explains in detail what steps have been taken in past years to ensure an adequate opening of the committee work in September and October. He then lists the chief objectives, emphases, and dates which were included by the former committee, with the assurance that these are merely for information and are not to determine the coming year's program of activities except in so far as the committee desires.

From time to time the minister should *compliment the leader on his achievements,* encourage him with appreciation and counsel, and make sure that he does not grow discouraged in his good work.

Likewise the minister should *publicize the leader and his work.* It is worth while to publish the names of all officials and heads of organizations with their personnel so that the entire church may know who are responsible for the various phases of its program and work. Because "names are news," the members will be interested in knowing who their officials are. The leaders themselves are pleased and honored at this recognition.

Sometimes it is necessary to *activate the inactive leader.* The failure of an officer in the church to discharge his duty is usually due to carelessness, oversight, or procrastination. Rarely is it due to deliberate and intentional neglect. Occasionally the cause is found in aging leadership which becomes too cautious and conservative for as important and dynamic a movement as the Christian church.

Most inert chairmen can be influenced either to become active or to resign with a minimum of friction. After carefully thinking through every possible phase of the work of the committee, the minister should talk with the inactive chairman, first inviting suggestions and then contributing his own. Make the task so large and important that the chairman will either be challenged to active leadership or discouraged into resigning. State tactfully but definitely that a meeting of the committee is necessary that its work may not be neglected. Agree with him on a date and a place, perhaps offering the pastor's home for an evening meeting. Talk with two or three members of the committee, discussing its task and planning constructive ideas. Help guide the conversation in the meeting and co-operate to the utmost with the chairman in activating the committee.

If these measures prove inadequate, suggest that because the chairman is too busy to carry all the load, a vice-chairman be appointed to help. It is often possible without friction to appoint an indifferent chairman to another committee where his inactivity will create less confusion and do less harm. It is sometimes wise to create a new committee position for this purpose. In extreme cases, where the chairman is both incompetent and un-co-operative, it becomes necessary to relieve him of his position. This should never be done until all other alternatives have failed.

A limited tenure of office or a rotating plan of filling official positions might seem to solve many of these difficult and delicate questions. To dislodge some obstinate or recalcitrant brother, churches have adopted a plan where no laymen can hold a chairmanship or official position longer than three years, with the added provision that he is ineligible to re-election for one or two additional years. Advantages claimed for this method are that it gets rid of those who do their work poorly; that it works more laymen into the tasks of the church; that it introduces new ideas into committees and organizations; and that it prevents two or three men from "holding all the offices."

Before the rotating system of choosing officials is adopted by any church, the disadvantages of the plan should be frankly faced. Among them are that able men with their talents and experience are automatically dropped; that chairmen must give up their leadership just when they are beginning to be really valuable; that certain areas of church life require a longer tenure of office for real efficiency; that the limiting of the term of office is artificial and arbitrary, based on the calendar rather than on the quality of the work done; that some of the finest leaders are difficult to re-enlist, pleading, "I have served my time"; that the minister is required to train each year new leaders for one third of the official committees and organizations of the church; and that there is a strong tendency for a committee or board to have no continuing, long-range policy.

After having conscientiously used both methods, the rotating of office technique in one church for nine years and the continuing tenure method in another church for seventeen years, I unhesitatingly affirm that the careful choice and training of "the best man for the job," under the continuing tenure plan, is by far the better method of filling the official positions of the church.

SPECIMEN COMMITTEE REPORT
Lay Activities Committee, page 146

CHAPTER 8

How to Cultivate Continuous Evangelism

BASIC PRINCIPLES

1. Continuous evangelism will enable any church anywhere greatly to increase its membership and church attendance.
2. The winning of new converts to Christ and the reclaiming of indifferent members to a renewed loyalty are the chief evangelistic tasks of any church.
3. Evangelism is a co-operative enterprise in which minister and laymen must share.
4. Friendly visitation evangelism by trained laymen has been found by most churches to be the most successful evangelistic method.
5. A well-rounded program for evangelistic objectives, methods, and dates should be outlined for the entire year.
6. Every new convert and member must be carefully trained and securely built into the fellowship and life of the church.
7. A "Fellowship of Evangelism," sometimes called "The Fishermen's Club," should be a permanent part of the organization of every church.

IN THIS increasingly nomadic, mobile, and volatile period in American history a year-round program of continuous evangelism is indispensable to the life of any church. Because of its relation to church attendance, the church school, and church finances, it is quite impossible to over-estimate its importance. The strength, character, and size of present and future congregations will be determined by the thoroughness with which this recruiting task of the local church is done. The church that evangelizes will live; the church that fails to evangelize will gradually die.

To define the areas of church and community life in which evangelism operates is to reveal how completely present-day evangelism has outgrown the narrow, limited, emotional types of a few years ago. Among the chief purposes of modern evangelism, which reveal the growing place it occupies in church life, are the following:

To reclaim indifferent church members to a renewed loyalty

To relate church members who move to another community to some church

To persuade non-Christians to accept Jesus Christ as their Lord and Saviour

To persuade the children and young people of the church to make their Christian decision

To give adequate membership training to new converts and new members and to assimilate them into the life of the church

To transform group and community life in the spirit and pattern of Jesus Christ

To aid in enriching and deepening the Christian life of the entire congregation

In every evangelistic effort one must remember that everyone is an immortal soul who must be saved by faith in Jesus Christ, the Son of God.

No great word in the vocabulary of churchmen has grown more rapidly in stature and acceptability than has evangelism. It is indeed a far call from the high-pressure, emotional appeal of the traveling evangelist to the evangelistic partnership of ministers and laymen in a nation-wide crusade to win converts and to reclaim inactive members. The breadth and richness of the evangelistic movement is revealed in these seven chief types of techniques:

1. *Pulpit evangelism,* which includes evangelistic sermons by the minister, as well as preaching missions, evangelistic services, and radio preaching.

2. *Visitation evangelism,* with its wide use of trained Christian laymen, and personal interviews of all kinds for securing commitment or recommitment to Christ and the church.

3. *Educational evangelism,* which works through the church school and other teaching groups of the church.

4. *Church loyalty evangelism,* whose objectives are the reclamation and renewed loyalty of indifferent church members.

5. *Fellowship evangelism,* which encourages the prospect to become acquainted with the spirit and life of the church for a three- or six-month period before making his commitment to Christ.

6. *Social evangelism,* whose aim is to change group and community life and make it Christian.

7. *Family evangelism,* whereby all members of the home are united in Christ through daily prayer, graces, Bible reading, and daily family worship.

Whatever methods are used, there must be depth and thoroughness in this supremely important matter.

Strengthen the committee on evangelism by adding to its personnel a suitable number of the ablest and most representative members of the church. The type and caliber of those who compose the committee will not only decide the number of members won or reclaimed, but will also determine the strength of congregation the church will have across future years. Among the subjects to be discussed and the decisions to be made by this important committee are the following:

The meaning of church loyalty and evangelism

The percentage of church membership present on an average Sunday

The number won to Christ and the church during the past twelve months

The training and assimilation of these new members

The goals for the coming year in new members, in converts, and in church attendance

The holding of two church loyalty crusades, accenting every-Sunday attendance during October and during Lent

A visitation evangelism movement to win new converts and new members

A community-wide survey in co-operation with other churches, to locate unchurched families

The holding of a preaching mission or special evangelistic services

The outlining of a month-by-month evangelistic program for the coming year

Plan twelve months of evangelistic aims, goals, and events in order that every important and appropriate evangelistic feature may be included in the total program for the evangelistic year. While the following calendar of evangelistic events may be adjusted and arranged as desired by any minister or church, it does contain most of the important projects and events that should be included by any church in its schedule of evangelistic activities:

September
   Plan and organize the Church Loyalty Crusade of church-wide visitation.

Choose and instruct the crusade visitors.

Observe Rally Day throughout the church, the church school, and youth groups.

Launch the Church Loyalty Crusade.

October

Announce and celebrate World Communion Sunday.

Encourage every-Sunday church attendance throughout October.

Make preparations for the Visitation Evangelism Crusade.

Assemble a large prospect list of all non-members of the congregation.

Select and enlist the evangelistic workers.

November

Open the Visitation Evangelism Crusade.

Receive the Thanksgiving class of new members after personal counsel and training.

Organize a Fellowship of Evangelism for continuous evangelistic calling.

January

Accent rededication and renewed loyalty to Christ and his church.

Hold Decision Day services in the appropriate departments of the church school.

Begin training the class in church membership.

February-April

Feature Lent as a period of growing Christlikeness and deepened spiritual life.

Hold another Visitation Evangelism Crusade, climaxing before Holy Week.

Receive a great Palm Sunday–Easter class of new members.

May

Call together the committee on evangelism to lay plans for the next twelve months.

Strengthen and enlarge the permanent Fellowship of Evangelism of competent lay workers, including young people, for continuous evangelistic visitation.

Fortunately, churches of all communions no longer regard a yearly series of protracted meetings or a single visitation crusade as adequate to the evangelistic task and opportunity before them. In tens of thousands of congregations a permanent fellowship of trained visitors gives from one to four evenings each month to this important task. In one large church no one can remain a member of this aggressive group unless he makes an average of four calls each month. At their monthly meetings these enthusiastic representatives of Jesus Christ share their experiences, receive additional instruction, accept their calling assignments for the coming month, and enjoy a rare fellowship unsurpassed by any other organization in the church. The joy they experience in this kingdom task is radiant, in part because they see lives become Christ centered. They see lonely people finding good friends and new members steadily welcomed into the church. As they share their faith with others, their own faith grows and glows.

Many new techniques have been devised for training evangelistic workers in recent years. Folders with specific "sales talks" and "effective appeals" have been supplemented with books that are admirably suited to a five- or six-week training course for workers. Phonograph records vividly dramatize the call, the conversation, and the signing of the decision card. A filmstrip has been produced by some denominational departments of evangelism, while the Methodist Board of Evangelism has produced a large turnover chart of 117 sheets, "They Went Forth Two by Two," which is now in general use by several denominations. All these helps vastly increase the interest and effectiveness of all who call.

Young people readily respond to the challenge of calling on those of similar age and interests in the interests of Christ and his church. Larger churches select from three to seven or eight teams of two each to combine in their calling the appeal of Christ and the church with a cordial invitation to join their youth group or fellowship. In many parts of the country they carry the evangelistic spirit and message to smaller communities where their visit has often meant transformed lives and renewed spiritual interest among youth.

Interest church-school teachers in evangelism as an integral part of their privilege and responsibility as leaders of children, young people, and adults. Under the slogan "Every Church-School Teacher an Evangelist" most of the denominational boards of education recognize that a definite commitment to Christ and a decision to unite with the Christian church are indispensable parts of any adequate program of Christian education. Because of his close contact and friendship with class members, the teacher is in an admirable position to lead his pupils to Christ. Cordially co-operating with the minister in preparation for Decision Day, the Christian teacher can play a leading role in the evangelistic drama.

Train converts and new members. When properly trained they appreciate the supremely important step they are taking. The instruction and indoctrination of new Christians represent an all too frequently unused Christian opportunity of crucial importance. The first step in this course of Christian training will be the minister's spiritual guidance visit after the Christian decision has been made. He will seek to confirm and strengthen the decision; to explain what is involved in being a Christian and a church member; to meet the religious needs and to give counsel concerning Christian habits, such as daily prayer, every-Sunday church attendance, Christian stewardship, and the reading of God's Word daily; and to indicate the time and place for the class of instruction in church membership.

Most churches now wisely require a membership training period of from three months to three years, conducted by the minister of the church. Instruction about God, the Creator and heavenly Father; Jesus Christ the Son of God and the Saviour of the world; the heroic history of the Christian church across the centuries; the rise of one's own communion; the growth of the ecumenical movement; the meaning and obligations of the Christian life; the Christlike habits of daily living; and the organization, life, and fellowship of the church assure permanence and spiritual growth. Those churches of all communions that are most successful in satisfactorily relating new members to the church encourage each new member:

To unite with some church-school class
To make a generous pledge to the church
To undertake some personal service for the church
To be present at the services of worship every Sunday
To win some friend to Christ and to the church
To accept and counsel with "the fellowship friend" who acts
  as his sponsor during the first year of his membership

Reclaim inactive members through a Church Loyalty Crusade. Three seasons of the Christian year admirably lend themselves to the cultivation of church loyalty and every-Sunday attendance. They are: *the month of October,* beginning with World Communion Sunday, when churches of nearly all communions urge their members to be present at the services of worship every Sunday in October, which they designate as "Church Loyalty Month";

the new year, when, starting with the first Sunday of January, all members of the church are encouraged to "Attend Church Every Sunday Through Easter"; *the Lenten season,* when "Attend Church Every Sunday in Lent" is held before the congregation as the privilege and obligation of every member of the church.

A year-round loyalty movement has aims that are much broader than the worthy objective of getting the saints out of bed and into their pews on Sunday morning. It seeks to deepen the love and loyalty of every Christian to Jesus Christ. It tries to lift the spiritual level of the individual and of the church. It attempts to persuade the indifferent, careless Christian to take his Christian obligation seriously. It tries to spread the blessings of Christian worship and fellowship to all members of the congregation. It strives "to seek and to save" those who have strayed from the fold of Christ.

The organization of the loyalty crusade and the selection of competent visitors follow closely the general outline proposed for the visitation evangelism crusade. Pamphlets and books listing in detail the successful appeals and practical techniques used in loyalty crusades are procurable from any denominational headquarters.

With immortal tidings in our mortal hands, let us say unto the people that they go forward throughout the year in a continuous and effective program of Christian evangelism.

SPECIMEN COMMITTEE REPORTS

CHAPTER 9

How to Increase Christian Giving

BASIC PRINCIPLES

1. Every congregation has untapped financial resources adequate for all its necessary work.
2. Christian stewardship, cultivated through sermons, teaching, and literature, offers the only firm foundation for continuous, generous giving.
3. An annual Loyalty Campaign or Every-Member Canvass should be held in every church, preceded by a period of information and inspiration.
4. Special offerings at appropriate seasons have a rightful place in the financial program of every church.
5. Every member of the church and church school should make some gift, large or small, in support of the work of the church.
6. The congregation must be kept informed concerning the financial condition and needs of the church.

MONEY for worthy causes, such as the church and Christian missions, is easy to raise in large amounts in any parish. If the funds are not forthcoming, it is because of faulty and unbusinesslike methods used by the leaders of the church. The resources are there waiting to be tapped by carefully planned, attractive publicity, and courteous, persistent persuasion. "Ask, and it shall be given you; seek, and ye shall find; knock, and it shall be opened unto you."

Any church of any size, anywhere, that cultivates Christian stewardship, that attractively presents its program of Christian service, and that extends to every member of the

96

church and church school a cordial and urgent personal invitation to share generously in the work of God through giving will find sufficient funds for all its local and missionary projects.

An understanding of present-day trends in church finance will help guide any local finance committee in the selection of areas and aims that will be financially productive. The successful experiences of churches of all sizes proves that when they include these new approaches and methods with their financial techniques, they have no difficulty whatever in providing funds for all their activities. Among these important trends are the following:

The year-round cultivation of Christian stewardship in preaching, teaching, and practice

The broadening of the financial base by persuading more and more members to pledge

The securing of many small pledges

The encouraging of boys and girls to pledge as their parents do

The holding of a Loyalty Sunday service for voluntary pledging

The shifting of the date of the budget campaign to October or November

A strong accent on Christian missions

The holding of simultaneous campaigns in all churches of a community in November

The liquidation of mortgages and other debts

The building of endowments, that loyal members may continue to share in God's work across the years

Projects that embody these trends greatly help churches in meeting any adverse conditions that result from general business conditions, increased costs, or keener competition with other religious and philanthropic organizations for a gift-dollar.

Emphasize stewardship throughout the church. Christian stewardship is partnership with God in investing one's life, time, talent, and means for the service of mankind in the spirit of Christ. "All that I am, all that I have, all that I know, and all that I do, I dedicate to God for his use," says the Christian steward. Far richer than money or tithing, stewardship is a romantic, thrilling, world-changing word.

Composed of representative men and women who take their Christian privileges seriously, the stewardship committee will first assemble all the stewardship literature which its denomination provides. This includes books, pamphlets, and articles that may be had free for distribution throughout the congregation. The minister will preach one or two effective stewardship sermons during the year on such themes as "The Sharing Life," "As God Has Prospered You," and "A Christian Philosophy of Life." He will exalt tithing and other forms of Christian stewardship by his example as well as by his preaching. At one service he will give the opportunity for the enrollment of those who will share as Christian stewards of their time, talent, and means. Throughout the church school, worship services, exhibits, and instruction will bring to all the joy and duty of sharing. A Christian conscience will be created concerning the use of life and the generous sharing of possessions.

Young people and children in the church school should be taught to share. No plan of Christian education is adequate that fails to cultivate the Christian habit of service and sacrifice. The Christian life always becomes introverted unless it expresses its Christlike love in sacrificial giving. The church-school teachers and parents have in their hands the keys that open the doors of dedi-

cation to growing personalities. Let them plan lessons
and worship services that feature sharing. Let them instruct
children and youth in the value and practical use of money.
Let them employ the eye-gate of visual education as well
as the Bible memory verses on sharing. Let them set up a
youth budget plan, such as the Presbyterian Church,
U.S.A., employs, as a strategy in churchmanship among
young people. Let them show children and youth what
their gifts accomplish, and let them help classes and individuals in choosing interesting projects of Christian
service.

The wisest possible financial strategy among children
and youth is found in the rapidly growing custom of encouraging all children and young people of the church
school to make an annual pledge *to their church* at the
time the budget is raised and to pay that pledge through
weekly envelopes. The value of cultivating the every-
Sunday habit of sharing cannot be overestimated. The tiny
gift of a nickel or a dime will grow across the years into a
handsome contribution. Children delight in pledging and
paying as their parents do. They also feel more completely
a part of the church which they help support.

Plan a church-wide financial campaign. Any church
that intelligently plans its budget-raising campaign and
thoroughly follows through will be amazed at the results.
Among the necessary steps in organizing and launching
the annual financial effort are the following:

1. *Appoint a strong campaign committee* composed of
the ablest men and women in the church, with a chairman
who possesses qualities of outstanding leadership and enthusiasm. To spread the responsibility four or more sub-
committees such as the following are appointed: (*a*) The
budget committee, which will examine the financial

records of the closing year, will survey the needs and opportunities of the coming year, and will recommend the current and missionary budget to the congregation. (*b*) The publicity committee, which will study appeals, prepare letters and folders, and formulate such plans as will inform the congregation and kindle enthusiasm. (*c*) The larger gifts committee, which will interview the larger givers, as well as those who ought to be larger givers, and will do so *before* the general solicitation begins. (*d*) The canvass committee, which will be large enough to call on all members of the church who do not make their pledges at the church services.

2. *Set challenging goals* for the congregation, both in the total amount to be subscribed and in the number of pledges to be made. While each succeeding budget will probably be larger than its predecessor in order to care for the expanding work of the church, this budget must never be padded. An honest budget that can be presented and defended in all its items creates confidence. An inflated budget undermines confidence because it is dishonest.

A study, year after year, of the increase in the number of pledges is necessary to any permanent rise in the total giving of a congregation. Influenced by the program of stewardship cultivation to regard more seriously one's obligation, the nonpledging members in larger numbers will join the ranks of their pledging fellow members. In a single year a church of five hundred members increased the number of its pledgers from 130 to 185 by persistently striving to achieve its campaign goal of 180 pledgers. The next step was to lift the goal to 205 for the following year. "Some pledge, large or small, from every member of the church" was the slogan adopted for the campaign.

3. *Prepare a personal pledge card* on which each mem-

6758

ber may record his generous pledge. Churches everywhere
are abandoning the cold, legal pledge form which begins,
"In consideration of the gift of others, etc.," and are sub-
stituting in its place the following, "Because of my love
for Christ and my church, and because I want to share with
my fellow Christians in prospering Christ's work, etc."
The following simple pledge form has been found effective.

MY PLEDGE TO CHRIST AND TO MY CHURCH
For Christ's Work Through My Church

To express my love to Christ and to my church, and
to help prosper the gospel and the world-wide mission
work of my church, I pledge the following for the financial year from November 1, 19__ to October 31, 19__.

FOR CURRENT EXPENSE $_____per week

FOR MISSIONS AND OTHER $_____per week
      BENEVOLENCES $_____per month

                             $_____per year

Signature _____

Increasing numbers of churches use the back of the pledge
card to list four or five of the chief reasons why one
should pledge.

4. *Write persuasive publicity* in the form of illustrated
and printed or duplicated folders and letters. Many
churches find that two mailings are most effective. The
first, ten days before the campaign opens, deals with the

work of the church, the missionary program, the church-school work among youth, and other features of the church's service. The second folder or letter stresses the privilege and duty of every member to make some pledge to the church and includes the budget for the coming year and information concerning the pledge card, the Victory Sunday service, and other financial matters. *It is a tragic mistake to mail the pledge card to the members.*

Inform the congregation fully concerning the varied types of Christian service rendered by their church. Alert churches find it sound policy and excellent strategy to re-think and resell the total program of the church to the entire congregation once each year. To acquaint each member with the achievements of the closing year as well as with the enlarged plans and new projects of the coming year maintains interest, extends knowledge, and increases giving. The members of any church have the right to know what their gifts have already accomplished and what their future contributions will be spent for during the coming year.

5. *Hold a Victory Sunday service,* which the entire membership is urged to attend, so that they may sign their pledges as an act of worship. Thousands of large and small churches raise from 50 to 85 per cent of their total budgets at the Victory Sunday morning service. Key-note this service to high inspiration and devotion. Make loyalty, victory, and the greatness of God's work the domi-nant note. Select jubilant marching hymns. Preach for a financial decision worthy of the work of the church and adequate to the immense needs of this broken world. Con-duct the pledging service at the close of the sermon by asking the ushers to distribute the pledge cards, by lead-ing the congregation in reading and signing these pledge

cards, and in placing them after they are signed at the foot of the cross on the Communion table or altar. Those who fail to make their pledges on Victory Sunday are then solicited by the canvassers, who have been chosen and trained in the effective presentation of the work and claims of the church. A friendly call on every nonpledging member will, when proper preparation has been made, increase the number of members pledging and lift the total giving of any church.

The problem of keeping pledges paid up to date is one that can be easily solved by the use of proper methods. Many churches now send every three months what is called "The Quarterly Settlement Reminder" to all who are one month or more in arrears on their pledges. These are in letter form similar to the following and, far from being resented, are welcomed by practically everyone:

An effective line in the weekly bulletin of one church reads as follows: "Fill your contribution envelope every Saturday evening and bring it with you to church on Sunday."

Special occasions, such as the end of the financial year, the closing of the vacation period, and the beginning of the new year, offer a natural opportunity as well as an urgent occasion for pledgers to bring their unpaid pledges to the church. Some churches make a weekly report of income and expenditures, placing this record before the congregation in their bulletin.

Secure large special offerings at appropriate seasons. The real and proper place which Thanksgiving, Christmas, Easter, and similar special offerings should have in the life of the church has been perverted and corrupted by far too many special appeals. Some pulpits have become the collection agencies for numerous causes, most of them

THE QUARTERLY SETTLEMENT DAY REMINDER

January 15, 19___

DEAR FELLOW MEMBER OF FIRST CHURCH:

As the end of the first three months of the new financial year approaches I am sending to all who pledge to the church and have unpaid balances this friendly Quarterly Settlement Day Reminder.

This is done always for two reasons: first, so that any mistakes in crediting gifts may be corrected, and second, so that First Church may secure funds to pay in full all her obligations for this first quarter, which ends January 31. If there should be any error, be sure to let me know.

According to my records, your pledge *as of the end of January* stands as follows:

DUE ON CURRENT EXPENSE $_____

DUE ON MISSIONS AND OTHER BENEVOLENCES $_____

If everyone who can will bring his gifts this coming Sunday or the following one, which is the last Sunday of the quarter, I believe we shall have enough to meet all our bills.

"It is so easy when everybody helps."

Yours in God's service,

_____

Finance Secretary

worthy, to the detriment of true worship and great preaching. Too often they have become a plague and an irritation. It is not the lifting of special offerings to which objection is made by a patient long-suffering congregation; it is the abuse of this good practice that is condemned.

The wise finance committee of any local church will list those causes to which the church ought to contribute during the coming year. The amount that each cause should expect from the congregation is then determined, together with the Sunday or season when the appeal should be made. Several causes can and should share in the same special offering in an amount appropriate to the needs and importance of the cause. While this technique is often unsatisfactory to the executives of philanthropic organizations, it is eminently desirable from the standpoint of the spiritual life of the church. Most churches that have considered the matter are convinced that five or six special offerings each year, in addition to the regular campaign for pledges, represent the greatest number that should be taken.

Maintain the financial health of the church. Here are a few methods:

1. *Solicit pledges from new members* within one week after they join the church. Having promised to contribute to the church, new members are often amazed at the neglect of the finance committee in failing to provide either contribution envelopes or pledge cards for them. Churches of many communions have found that the writing of a friendly form letter, explaining the financial plan of the church, followed by the mailing of a package of envelopes and a call by one of the members of the finance committee with a pledge card, results in practically one hundred per cent pledging. New members respect the businesslike management of their church when these financial matters are handled in a prompt, systematic manner.

2. *Conduct a midyear canvass* at the end of the first six months of the financial year. Many members who find it impossible to pledge at the time of the annual campaign find their circumstances entirely changed after the passing of four or five months. Doctor bills have been paid, employment has been found, and other obligations have been met. When visited by persuasive canvassers, nonpledging members will often contribute an amount equal to from 3 to 6 per cent of the budget as a result of the midyear solicitation. This movement has the additional advantage of making it easier for them to continue their pledges at the time of the next canvass.

3. *List the chief events of the financial year* in order that every phase of stewardship cultivation and financial harvest may be given its proper place. Assuming that the financial year opens on December 1, the following outline will indicate most of the important movements and events related to the financial health of the local church:

December
  1st Sunday: Dedication of pledges
  3rd Sunday: Christmas Sunday sermon; Christmas offering
February
  15: First Quarterly Settlement Reminders
  2nd Sunday: Preparation for a plan of experimental tithing
    during Lent
  3rd Sunday: Stewardship sermon
Lenten Period (opening on Ash Wednesday and climaxing
    on Easter Day) Encouragement of Christian stewardship
    throughout Lent; Lenten–Holy Week self-denial offering
May
  1st Sunday: Stewardship Sunday; signing of stewardship
    and enrollment cards

15: Second Quarterly Settlement Reminders; launching of mid-year canvass

June

2nd Sunday: Children's or Students' Day offering

3rd Sunday: Bulletin announcement about paying pledges during vacation

August

15: Third Quarterly Settlement Reminders

September

2nd Sunday: Bulletin announcement about the payment of pledges now vacation is over

October

1st Sunday: Rally Day offering in the church school

1st week: Preparations for the church budget campaign to be held in November

2nd Sunday: Bulletin announcement about bringing pledges up to date

November

2nd Sunday: Launching of annual pledging campaign; Victory Sunday service of pledging

3rd Sunday: Visitation of all who have not yet pledged

3rd week: Financial letter reminding members of close of financial year, November 30

4th Sunday: Distribution or mailing of the boxes of contribution envelopes

The above schedule of important events in the financial year can easily be adapted to any church by simply adjusting it to any month or season that best suits the custom or judgment of the finance committee. Pledge Sunday, for instance, does not have to come in November as above suggested. Local plans can be determinative here.

Here are some other projects which will help keep the church in good financial health:

1. Elect a separate treasurer for each church fund in order that funds given for definite purposes may not be diverted

2. Make a master pledging file for the coming five years in order that the pledging record of each member may be easily placed before the estimating committee

3. Have all church financial records audited by a certified public accountant

4. Dedicate all pledges as a special feature of the morning service on the first Sunday of the new financial year

5. Encourage tithing as an experiment during the seven weeks of Lent or at any more convenient season

6. Form a stewardship guild composed of all Christian stewards

7. Select six pamphlets from those available at denominational stewardship headquarters and secure enough of them so that they may be distributed to the entire church and church school on the first Sunday of every second month of the year

8. Reprint short, attractive articles on stewardship in the weekly bulletin

9. Encourage the setting aside of "God's Acre" in rural communities

10. Pay off the church debt, if any

11. Start a permanent endowment fund and encourage gifts to it by members of the congregation

Specimen Committee Reports

Finance Committee, page 148
Endowment Committee, page 149
Christian Stewardship Committee, page 158

How to Expand Missions and Community Service

BASIC PRINCIPLES

1. Christian missions, today as always, rank as one of the most significant international movements in the world.
2. Missionary education lays a broad foundation for world peace and brotherhood.
3. The church that gives generously to missions always has ample funds for its local work.
4. Every church owes the world and its own community the gift of time, talent, and sacrificial service.
5. Unselfish service to one's community and one's world brings rich returns to the local church.

THE Christian church is largely responsible for much of the creative ferment in the world today. She has sent her missionaries everywhere, broadcasting the good news of Christ, liberty, and the abundant life. Mission schools that aroused discontent with ignorance and illiteracy became the forerunners of national school systems in backward countries. Mission churches have created a fellowship of Christ-minded people who have given hope to the under-privileged. The spirit of Christian freedom has helped dissolve caste systems and has aided in toppling tyrannies. Through Christian missions a newer, better, freer world is being born.

A rich, well-balanced, continuous program of missionary

information and inspiration is necessary if the members of the local church are to have a world vision in this world-minded age. To be parochial in outlook and introverted in interest are sins of omission of which no true Christian church or minister will be guilty.

With the newspapers full of world events and with the challenging threat of unchristian world movements before him, the minister has an unparalleled opportunity to urge his people in sermon and counsel to share the good news of Jesus Christ with all the world.

Organize for missions and community service. What a good roadbed is to a fast train, or a well-engineered concrete road is to a swift automobile, organization is to the local church. Create first of all a board or committee on Christian missions, composed of five to seven men, women, and young people who are or will become interested in world affairs. Among these would be the superintendent of missions of the church school and the president of the women's missionary group. Some of the major duties of this board would be:

1. A study of the missionary program of the denomination
2. The choice and distribution during the year of ten or twelve leaflets or folders on the church's mission fields at home and abroad
3. Co-operation with the board of education and the church school in missionary education
4. The holding of one or more World Vision evenings
5. The encouragement of increased giving to missions
6. The stimulation of missionary interest throughout the church in every possible way

Make missions interesting by visualizing and personalizing the Christian movement at home and abroad. The drama of color and race, as well as the difficult problems and desperate needs of the peoples of the world, prove fascinating to any congregations when ably presented. The Sunday evening services once each month offer an excellent opportunity for showing the beautifully colored slides and motion pictures which the missions boards of all denominations now provide. Some churches accent home missions during one year with such subjects as "Negroes in the United States," "The Migrant Problem," "Spanish-Speaking Americans," and "City Slums," while the next year, once each month, they make a "world tour" by presenting visually Christian missionary work in Japan, China, the Philippines, and other countries.

Missionaries home on furlough can often be secured for an evening to tell their amazing stories of service and redemption, as well as to exhibit costumes and articles of interest from their mission field. One church, two Sundays before pledge Sunday, displayed a large colored map of the world on which were located the missionaries and foreign mission projects supported by that church. The following year a map of the United States was shown, with the chief home missionary causes featured. These large maps, eight by sixteen feet, were made, drawn, and colored on sign cloth by a class of young people from the church school. Interesting letters from missionaries and news paragraphs concerning missionary events of interest should be included occasionally in the weekly bulletin. The distribution of pamphlets and folders about home and foreign missions is common practice on ten or twelve Sundays of the year at the church services and in the church school of most churches.

Feature themes of world-wide interest at World Vision evenings or Schools of Missions. World events now occupy a larger place in the news and in the minds of men than ever before. Churches that have announced such themes as the following, usually in connection with a fellowship family supper on Wednesday or Friday evenings, have rendered a signal service to large numbers of their members and constituents: "The United Nations Organization," "The World Council of Churches," "The Future of World Peace," "The Four Freedoms," "Self-Government Throughout the World," "Frank Laubach and World Literacy," "World Communism and World Christianity." A typical school of missions program appears on page 113.

Develop world vision in the church school. The great wealth of missionary material to be found in the lesson material for all ages prepared by each denomination affords a splendid opportunity for the promotion of missions in church-school worship periods and in class study and discussion. In the worship center of many church-school departments will be found a globe of the world, in addition to the Bible and the cross, symbolizing the unity of mankind and the obligation to go into all the world with the Christian gospel. Some schools devote one Sunday worship service each month to missions, the offering on that Sunday being devoted for some specific missionary project. Illustrated posters in color are created by some classes, while dramas and tableaux in costume by others present the missionary theme of the day. Pictures of the children of all nations adorn the walls as the worship leader, assisted by members of the department, relates the romantic story of missions in some needy land.

Probably the most vivid and creative missionary project which any group can sponsor is the "adoption" in some foreign or home mission field of a child or young person of the average age of the members of the department. One

St. John's Sixth Annual

CHURCH SCHOOL OF MISSIONS

Sunday Evenings: January 8, 15, 22, 29
  5:30—Supper in Social Hall (50¢)
  6:15—Movies for All the Family
  7:00-8:00—Interest and Discussion Groups for Adults,
    Young Adults, Youth Fellowship, and the Children's
    Division

Nursery and Kindergarten: "New Friends," led by Mrs. Peter
  Macken and Mrs. Hubert Wayne
Primary: "Children of New Japan," led by Mrs. O. L. Fox, Mrs.
  Oren Ballin, and Mrs. John Wexer
Junior: "Where the Car Banners Fly," led by Mrs. Robert
  Jayne, Mrs. Olive Harte, Mrs. Webster Olds, and Miss
  Louise Carr
Junior Hi Fellowship: "A New Look at Japan," led by Mrs.
  O. P. Weaver, Mrs. Harry Locke, Mrs. Patrick Dorr, and
  Mrs. Edwin Fish
Senior Hi and College Fellowship and The Sunday Evening
  Club have related programs
Adult Section: "Japan Begins Again," led by Dr. Hubert
  Wayne and Miss Mary Osaka

Textbook Sales and Library: Miss Jean Owen
Suppers: Women's Guild
Exhibits: Mrs. H. W. Moth
Movies: John Sweetman
Posters: Peter Knight, Olga Hay, Sara White

The school is sponsored by St. John's Board of Missions,
  Mrs. Howard Lang, chairman

junior department voted to accept the responsibility for the support of a ten-year-old boy in a mission school in India, securing his name from the board of missions. To him they wrote letters and sent Christmas gifts, and they received from him his picture and occasional letters. To this cause these juniors made genuinely sacrificial gifts until in about five months they had raised the sixty dollars necessary to support the boy for one year. The sponsorship and support of a native missionary is easily within the financial resources of an adult class or a youth or young adult department.

Increased gifts for missions will inevitably result from larger knowledge and heightened inspiration as the program of cultivation goes forward. Churches have found that the more they give to missions the more they have for themselves. Congregations have discovered that one of God's laws of church finance provides that the generous church is always the prosperous church. Among the scores of techniques for increasing missionary giving, these have been found by churches of many communions to be among the most successful:

1. An every-member canvass for missions, separate from the annual campaign for current expenses
2. A joint campaign for current and missionary funds, using a pledge card that affords each member an opportunity to make a separate, definite pledge for missionary work in addition to his pledge for local support
3. The receiving of a monthly missionary offering from all members of the church school
4. The support, in whole or in part, of a missionary in some home or foreign field
5. Frequent announcement, either from the pulpit or in the

weekly bulletin, of what the missionary money given by the congregation accomplishes

Any congregation anywhere can double its missionary giving without in any way reducing the amount that the congregation will give to local support.

Create a social action committee for community study and service in civic, moral, and religious matters. Most churches are organized primarily for their own ecclesiastical, religious, and missionary purposes, and they are all too rarely effective in their local influence and their service to their own community. Every local church profits greatly by community-wide contacts through a carefully selected committee as its representative in the growing field of interchurch co-operation. Such a Christian social action committee, composed of some of the wisest and ablest lay members of the church who command the confidence of both church and community, can be of inestimable value in applying the spirit and teachings of Jesus Christ to the perplexing problems of today. Among its chief duties will be:

1. To represent the church in its growing co-operation with other churches, through the local council of churches and other interdenominational groups
2. To help the church in its search for worth-while opportunities of community service and to recommend appropriate projects to church classes and organizations
3. To co-operate with other churches in turning the searchlight of fact and publicity on civic conditions that are vicious or evil
4. To influence and to aid civic and school authorities in matters that pertain to the welfare of the community
5. To help mold the thinking of the entire church on such

matters as war and peace, international co-operation, good government, individual responsibility in civic affairs, and other social, economic, and moral matters

Such a committee in every local church, meeting with similar committees from other churches to discover and express the Christian position on matters of social tension, such as bigotry, intolerance, group selfishness, delinquency, and crime, can render a notable service to the entire community.

The social action committee should recommend worthwhile community service projects to organizations in the church. Among the community projects church groups have found interesting and rewarding in the service they have rendered their neighborhoods are the following:

1. The sponsoring of a Boy Scout or Girl Scout Troop, or a 4-H Club
2. The entertainment of crippled children
3. The organization of a Teen-Age Canteen or a young people's club
4. The showing of good motion pictures in a community or neighborhood where there is no motion-picture theater
5. The leading of a campaign for clean motion pictures and clean literature, where conditions make this desirable
6. Aiding the Red Cross and hospitals in sewing, nursing, and in the blood donors' movement
7. Acting as Big Brothers to those paroled by the court
8. Encouraging all voters to register and to vote in every election
9. Commending public officials when they have discharged their duty well

The church that saves its life and its money will surely lose both, while the congregation that invests its talents and resources in Christian missions and community service will steadily prosper.

SPECIMEN COMMITTEE REPORTS

CHAPTER 11

How to Co-operate with Other Churches

BASIC PRINCIPLES

1. It is a primary duty of every church and every minister to co-operate in the spirit of Christ with other churches.
2. The Protestant churches of the United States are rapidly standardizing their programs and uniting their forces in a long-range strategy for Christian fellowship and service.
3. Increasing numbers of kingdom tasks can be far more effectively done by united effort through a council of churches or a ministers' union than by individual churches alone.
4. Interchurch co-operation expresses in part the Christian answer to Christ's prayer, "That they may all be one."

THE Protestant churches are uniting! In the true American tradition, like the thirteen colonies, the Protestant communions have voluntarily drawn together that they might form a more perfect union in Christian fellowship, more firmly establish the kingdom of God, and promote the cause of Christ at home and abroad. They have organized councils of churches, created a literature of Christian union, worked out programs of Christian service at home and abroad, developed strategies and techniques, and have worshiped and worked together in the spirit of Christ. This unitive movement is the outstanding fact in the religious life of the United States today. It will increasingly affect and mold the program of every evangelical church in the country.

To grasp the significance and scope of this interchurch movement for the local church one must contrast the timid, tentative, unofficial conversations prior to 1900 with the amazing growth and strength of Christian unity today. There are now 838 state, city, and local councils of churches, 214 of which employ professional executive leadership. More than 1,500 ministerial associations have been organized by ministers, while the Christian women of the United States have created about 1,600 local councils of church women. The supreme achievement of this unitive spirit is expressed in the new National Council of the Churches of Christ in the U.S.A., which draws together in one great council the missionary, educational, evangelistic, and interchurch co-operative movements among the Protestant denominations of the country. The creation of this great council by voluntary, unforced fellowship in Christian worship and service is infinitely more impressive than any monolithic religious authoritarianism can ever be.

Understand the interchurch movement. One can sense these important trends in American Protestantism today as they constructively affect the life of tens of thousands of local churches:

Toward a united awareness and appreciation of the Protestant Christian heritage

Toward exalting the church as the fellowship of all believers

Toward emphasizing the points of fundamental agreement among the communions which vastly outweigh the items of incidental difference

Toward cordial co-operation in areas of mutual interest, such as home and foreign missions, evangelism, Christian education, and stewardship

Toward the reunion of the branches of a given communion

Toward the organic union of separate denominations

Toward the federation or merging of smaller churches in overchurched communities

Toward standardizing and synchronizing schedules, programs, and emphases on both national and local levels

Toward united action on moral, civic, and ecclesiastical matters

Toward co-operation in weekday religious education

Toward interdenominational religious surveys of local communities

Toward a uniformity of methods in the united raising of the budgets of the churches of a community

Toward an enriched and more uniform Christian church year

Toward ecumenicity as expressed in the World Council of Churches and in the concept of the Holy Christian Church

Toward the pooling of experience and judgment in the practical work of the local church

Toward more reverent, beautiful services of worship and toward more churchly architecture

Toward union services, such as those held on Reformation Day, during Lent, and on Good Friday

Toward the interdenominational training of ministers

Toward the extension of the scope and powers of interdenominational organizations

Toward united and effective opposition to proposals that threaten religious liberty or weaken the separation of church and state

These trends are phases of an interchurch movement in which every church must share if it is to perform its ministry adequately.

Form a pastors' union or a federation of churches to express and increase the basic unity and community of interest of all churches throughout the church year. A divided Protestantism is weak in the face of the tensions and pressure groups of current civic and social life. A united Protestantism in the power of its Christian convictions can work wonders in its impact on the civic and moral life of the community.

The organization of a pastors' union or ministerial association is a comparatively simple matter. Recognizing their mutual interest and their common problems, let several ministers get together to explore the areas, opportunities, activities, and problems which they have in common. As they do so, they will find that misunderstandings and jealousies are dissipated while differences and frictions are dissolved. Besides sharing their professional interests and enjoying their mutual fellowship, they will find that on all matters affecting the welfare of their community they unitedly possess far greater power than they realize.

The formation of a federation or council of churches in any county or community involves a more elaborate organization and a more careful procedure. In addition to including both laymen and ministers, any council or federation will be constituted on a representative basis through officially elected delegates. Among the customary steps in organizing a council will be found the following:

1. Two or three ministers, each with a leading layman of his congregation, spend an evening thinking through the values, needs, activities, and organization of the proposed council.

2. They write to the state Council of Churches for folders and suggestions, as well as for guidance and help, in outlining and launching the council.

3. They call together a larger group, which includes all ministers of the community, together with one leading layman from each church, for discussion, suggestion, and

comment. This group appoints a committee to prepare a recommended constitution for the united effort.

4. At a great banquet or mass meeting of laymen and ministers of the community the constitution is presented, discussed, and approved.

5. Each church in the community then takes official action to enter or to remain outside the council. If its action is favorable, then it elects the number of delegates to which it is entitled.

6. These delegates then meet to perfect the council's formal organization by electing its officers and committee chairmen. Such a movement, in addition to having excellent publicity value for the Protestant forces of the community, helps to crystallize and unify the influence and fellowship of all the churches.

Pamphlets explaining more elaborately the organization and program of a pastors' union or a federation of churches can be procured from the state council of churches.

Such an organization can *outline a definite program of united service*. In this program the churches will join in serving their communities and themselves. Among the fruitful fields of co-operation on the community-wide level are:

1. The holding of union or simultaneous services at appropriate seasons of the year
2. A study of social conditions as they affect the civic, moral, and religious life of the community
3. The conducting of a friendly house-to-house survey to discover the unchurched residents in each neighborhood
4. A church loyalty month held in October to stimulate every-Sunday attendance
5. The raising of all church budgets at the same time

6. A visitation evangelism crusade for the winning of new members to all the churches
7. The sponsoring of leadership training schools for church-school teachers and officers
8. A study of underprivileged groups in the town or city

At appropriate times of the year it can *sponsor union or simultaneous services* by all the churches. The impact on the consciousness of the community created by the united observance of religious occasions is more strongly favorable to the churches than most of them realize. The average layman heartily approves and applauds such united Christian efforts as the causes featured on the following occasions:

> Labor Sunday
> Rally Sunday
> World Communion Sunday
> World Order Sunday
> Reformation Sunday
> Budget Sunday
> Thanksgiving Sunday
> Union Thanksgiving service
> Christmas Sunday and Christmas Eve
> Watchnight service
> World Day of Prayer
> Lenten or Holy Week services
> Good Friday three-hour service
> Easter Day
> Summer Sunday evening services

The pastors' union or federation of churches can *consider and discuss community conditions*. The combined strength of the interchurch approach is most clearly demonstrated whenever a co-operative Protestant organization starts to investigate and study the civic and moral conditions in the community. Public officials are always extremely sensitive to the strength of a united approach, and are justly afraid of a public opinion aroused by the religious forces of the city.

When the churches, which are usually too timid or are entirely silent on moral issues, get the facts concerning gambling, liquor law violations, and salacious literature, and correctly state them, they hold in their hands a terrific leverage for securing improved conditions. The wisest and most effective strategy is to lay the facts plainly before the government officials in charge, such as the mayor, the city manager, or the chief of police. The probabilities are that they will willingly co-operate in order to avoid unfavorable newspaper publicity. If they fail to act favorably, then the united voice of the churches of the community should be heard. One church can be ignored, but a number of congregations have too many votes for any political party to brush them aside.

It is worth while to *conduct a community-wide survey-study* in order to locate the unchurched families of the community at least once every three or four years. In every community there are hundreds of people who can be won to the fellowship of some Christian church. Some are members in other towns and cities, while many others can be brought for the first time into the church school or church fellowship. Children and young people in astounding numbers receive no regular Christian instruction in either Sunday school or church.

To discover all of these in a given neighborhood it is necessary to conduct a study-survey, in which all the churches should co-operate. After one such survey in the suburb of a large city, a church discovered more children and young people than it could possibly care for. Samples of the folder of instructions, the survey card, and the general interchurch organization for such a survey may be secured from any state council of churches or the department of evangelism of any communion.

After such a survey it is natural to *unite in a visitation evangelism crusade* for the winning of converts and new members. In the late autumn and during Lent churches are increasingly uniting in visitation evangelism movements by laymen to secure commitments to Christ and to his church. All communions now realize that trained laymen are highly effective in presenting the challenge of the Christian life and the obligation of membership in Christ's church. Most of them have found that much more than 50 per cent of the accessions to their churches have come from friendly calls by laymen in the homes of prospective members. During the last decade thousands of ministers have been trained to lead such crusades in communities of all sizes. In the usual four-day crusade period they train the selected laymen, instruct them in the techniques of presenting Christ and his church, and aid ministers in the important task of planning their membership training and assimilation program. When the evangelism crusades of the several churches are simultaneous, laymen are more readily enlisted for this task, while prospective members are more willing to make their commitments.

Another worthy project is to *conduct a church loyalty crusade* on an interchurch basis to secure every-Sunday church attendance. Publicity in the local newspapers will aid in making everyone church attendance conscious. Such slogans as "See You in Church Sunday" and "Come to Church Sunday" popularize the privilege and duty of regular worship. Nearly all the communions of the United

States have wisely chosen October as Church Loyalty Month and have provided excellent material for its proper observance.

More than a thousand communities *secure pledges simultaneously*. Their experience has more than justified their faith in the unitive technique in affairs financial. In November, when more money can be raised than in any other month of the year, they announce their budgets, make their appeals, train their lay canvassers, and unite in their newspaper appeal for support. With such slogans as "Everybody Caring and Everybody Sharing" they are given generous blocks of time on the radio and many columns of valuable space in the newspapers. They use all the successful techniques of persuasion which they formerly employed, but they find these heightened, strengthened, and more effective because of the undergirding publicity of the united effort. Full information concerning the organization and methods of the united church campaign may be secured by writing your state council of churches.

Work together for Christian education. Certain educational opportunities may be grasped by several churches in co-operation which would be beyond the means of a single church.

Two or more churches may *hold a leadership training school* for church-school teachers and officers. The master key that will open the door to improved Christian education is a well-trained church-school faculty. Their skills and talents will determine both the quality and instruction they give as well as the number who attend. An improved church school is possible only by improved church-school teachers. Few churches have the financial resources to provide three competent instructors for training the teachers of the children, youth, and adult departmental groups. Where, however, the children's instructor may be provided by the Methodists, the youth instructor by the Presbyterians, and the adult instructor by the Baptists from among their approved denominational leadership training personnel, the problem is easily and happily solved. An annual school of this kind is indispensable to the high type of Christian education every congregation deserves. In addition to increasing teaching skills and improving techniques, an interchurch leadership training course will markedly heighten morale.

Churches working co-operatively can *provide weekday Christian education* for public school pupils. There is little doubt that weekday religious instruction by well-trained Christian teachers is one of the most important "waves of the future" in American religious life. While court decisions have somewhat limited the place and time where such religious instruction may be given, the whole field of weekday religious education at other than public school hours is wide open.

Held in churches, such classes can not only splendidly supplement the excellent instruction given in Sunday school, but can also reach scores of girls and boys not connected in any way with any church or church school. In one Michigan community the entire church-school population in the fourth, fifth, sixth, and seventh grades, with their parents' permission, have for years received training in religious and moral matters. Any denominational board of education can give full information and helpful guidance in all weekday Christian educational matters.

Agree on principles of comity and co-operation in the establishment of new churches and in the relocation of old ones. Protestant strategy has all too frequently lagged far behind the expansion of modern American cities, due in part to denominational autonomy and to an absence of factual information and statesmanship. Fortunately today all leading Protestant communions have largely abandoned their former competitive attitude and are co-operating through comity committees. In both city and rural areas the principles of Christian comity, the techniques for studying a proposed church location, the consideration of population trends, and the several steps involved in the wise choice of a proper location are all to be found in pamphlets on church comity available at the office of any state council of churches.

Every local church whose minister is wise and whose laymen are alert will include a generous number of interdenominational activities in its planned program for every church year.

> In essentials, unity;
> In nonessentials, diversity;
> In everything, charity.

SPECIMEN COMMITTEE REPORTS

Co-operation Committee, pages 158-59
Christian Social Action Committee, page 159

A Specimen Church-wide Planning Conference Program

I̲f "one picture is worth ten thousand words," as the Chinese proverb aptly puts it, then the specimen program which follows may be of greater value than the main body of this book in making clear the technique of planning a year's work in the church.

This specimen represents the comprehensive program of one church which has used this method for eighteen years. Its content is substantially that of the original, but denominational and other activities not of general interest or application have been omitted, and fictitious names have been substituted except in a few cases which will be readily recognized. Although the program of some other church might have been selected from the scores available, this example was chosen because it covers the chief areas and activities which most American churches emphasize. Among these are preaching, worship, music, Christian education, youth work, missions, evangelism, church attendance, lay leadership, stewardship, finances, and others.

A notable feature of current Protestant church life is the rapidly growing similarity of the programs of Christian service on the local church level among most denominations. Because of this increasing unity and co-operation one can easily adapt the following reports to the situation of his own church by changing the names of several organizations and committees and by adding denominational emphases and activities. Any church, large or small, in any communion, should find in this specimen much helpful suggestion for planning the year's work and working the year's plans.

The reports which follow were prepared by the various committees and organizations during the month of May as plans and recommendations for the year beginning in September. All the reports were collected, and copies were mailed in a single booklet to all officers and committee chairmen as a prospectus for the Church-wide Planning Conference in early June. Space was provided under each report for the individual to jot down his own suggestions for amendments or additions to be discussed in the conference.

ACHIEVEMENTS OF THE CLOSING YEAR

1. The Church School has increased in average attendance to 467, a gain of 47 per Sunday.

2. The New Site has been enlarged by the purchase of an additional lot.

3. The architect has been commissioned to go forward in preparing final floor plans and working drawings for the New Edifice so that bids may be secured from contractors.

4. Fellowship Family Night attendance has averaged nearly 400.

5. The Seventy, a congenial group of couples and individuals, has been organized for regular, every-month evangelism, and has already achieved excellent results during the winter and spring.

6. Sixty laymen have been chosen as ushers to serve for two months each at the Sunday morning service.

7. The responsibility for the work of the church has been much more widely spread during the year by the appointment of about thirty more younger men and women to the official committees of the church.

8. Attendance at the morning services has been larger and steadier than in many years.

9. The pledges totaled $2,686.76 more than the previous year, and the special offerings for missionary and benevolent causes increased 20 per cent.

10. Probably the outstanding achievement of the year has been the steady growth and improvement in the everyday, regular work of the church.

OBJECTIVES FOR THE COMING YEAR

1. To win for Christ and his church at least 200 new members during the year

2. To work for an average Church School attendance of 525, with the possible establishment of two new adult classes

3. To secure working drawings and bids from contractors for the New Edifice

4. To encourage 1,300 to take Communion on October 1, World Communion Sunday

5. To organize a Youth Choir in the early autumn

6. To cultivate gifts and bequests to the New Edifice and to the Endowment Fund, as has been done for a number of years

7. To observe October as Church Loyalty Month, with a goal of "Every Member Present Every Sunday"

8. To spread even more widely the tasks of the church

9. To enlarge and intensify the youth work of the church

10. To reorganize the Parish Group Plan, dividing the entire membership of the church into geographical groups, each with a leader for calling, friendship, and service

THE CHRISTIAN YEAR IN
PREACHING AND WORSHIP

The sermons and services for the coming year will accent "The Church"—churchmanship, loyalty, every-Sunday church attendance, the ministry, Christian vocation, the priesthood of all believers, and a growing Christian experience. Evangelism will be the pervading and undergirding spirit of the year.

Appropriate hymns have been chosen for the year, no hymn being used more than once in the morning services and none more than once in the evening services. The Children's Choir will sing their "Hymn of the Month," which they study and memorize, on the third Sunday of each month.

The girls and boys, who attend the morning service in large numbers, will receive a three-minute children's sermon each Sunday before they go out to their expanded Church School session during the last forty-five minutes of the morning service.

Features of the evening services, held each Sunday evening at 7:30 from September through Easter, will include evangelistic sermons, illustrated missionary travelogues with colored slides and motion pictures, guest preachers, religious music by choirs, religious or biblical dramas, and occasional social evenings.

The ministers will exercise complete freedom in changing any sermon theme or subject as may be deemed desirable because of changing conditions. While about one in seven was changed last year, the following subjects chart the main course of the preaching and worship for the months that lie ahead.

SEPTEMBER

3 *Labor Sunday*
   M. "The Master of All Good Workmen," hymns 118, 293; broadcast

10 *Return Sunday*
   M. "God's Unfinished Business," hymns 17, 287; welcoming of

September class of new members; September baptismal service; first autumn appearance of the Chorus Choir

E. "The Joy of Religion," hymns 50, 212, 12

17 M. "Sir, We Would See Jesus," hymns 164, 238
E. "New Frontiers of Faith," hymns 44, 270, 256

24 *Rally Day—Christian Education Sunday*
M. "America Needs Christian Character," hymns 266, 255; dedicatory service opening the intensive Christian educational year at which the Board of Education and all the Church School teachers, associate teachers, and officers will sit together
E. "Christian Living in Tense Times," hymns 396, 56, 303

OCTOBER—Church Loyalty Month

1 *World Communion Sunday,* opening of Church Loyalty Crusade of five Sundays, "Every Member Present and Taking Communion"
M. "One Church in Christ," hymns 1, 411; Communion service; welcoming of October class of new members; broadcast
E. "The Things That Cannot Be Shaken," hymns 47, 315, 198

8 *World Vision Sunday,* second Sunday of the Loyalty Crusade
M. "The New Christian World Movement," hymns 475, 484; October baptismal service; probable visit from our missionary in China, Dr. Joseph Winthrop
E. "This Is China," illustrated with colored slides and motion pictures

15 *Loyalty Sunday,* "Every Member Present and Pledging Generously"
M. "The Church Faces the World," hymns 280, 379
E. "Toward a Christian Community," hymns 354, 249, 460

22 *Stewardship Sunday*
M. "The Greatest in the Kingdom," hymns 279, 259
E. "What Are You Living For?" hymns 543, 330, 483

29 *Reformation Sunday*
M. "The Faith of a Protestant Christian," hymns 67, 24
E. "The Freedom of the Sons of God," hymns 379, 228, 533

NOVEMBER

5 First Sunday of the City-wide Evangelistic Crusade

M. Opening of the Preaching Mission, with a distinguished guest preacher, hymns 253, 293; welcoming of November class of new members; dedication of loyalty pledges; broadcast

E. The Preaching Mission, continued

12 Climax of the City-wide Evangelistic Crusade

M. The Preaching Mission, concluded; November baptismal service

3:30 P.M.   Great evangelistic rally in the Masonic Auditorium, with distinguished guest preacher and massed choirs

19 *Thanksgiving Sunday*

M. "Present-Day Pilgrims," hymns 545, 20

E. "In Everything Give Thanks," hymns 24, 162, 67

26 M. "Signs of High Hope," hymns 337, 4

E. "Spanish-speaking America," illustrated with colored slides and motion pictures, hymns 475, 219, 259

DECEMBER

3 *First Sunday in Advent, National Council of Churches Sunday*

M. "The United Church of the United States," a sermon featuring the National Council of the Churches of Christ in the U.S.A., hymns 381, 89; welcoming of Crusade class of new members; broadcast

E. "A New Day for Christianity," hymns 302, 225, 381

10 *Universal Bible Sunday*

M. "The Word of God," hymns 386, 387

E. A Christmas drama, "A Child Is Born," presented under the direction of the Drama and Pageantry Committee, hymn 89

17 *Woman's Society Sunday*

M. Mrs. J. D. Welcombe, guest speaker, with members of the Woman's Society, the Forty-four Chapter, and the Service Guild sitting in a body, hymns 111, 479

E. Christmas music by the Chorus Choir and Quartet, hymn 100

24 *Christmas Sunday*

M. "God's Gift to You," hymns 86, 106; Christmas baptismal service

11:00 P.M. Christmas Eve Midnight Service, "A Star, a Song, and a Babe," special music by the Youth Choir, hymns 11, 89, 87

31 *Old Year Sunday*
    M. "The Good That This Year Has Brought," hymns 487, 239
    11:00 P.M. Watchnight Communion service

JANUARY

 7 *New Year Sunday*
    M. "This Can Be a Better Year," hymns 278, 240; welcoming
    of January class of new members; broadcast
    E. "The Long Look at Life," hymns 301, 145, 520

14 M. Sermon by our Canadian exchange preacher, Dr. John R.
    Webster, who has for the past four years exchanged pulpits
    with the pastor on this Sunday, hymns 510, 167; January
    baptismal service
    E. Address by Dr. Webster at a great city-wide rally

21 M. "This Disturbing Christ of Ours," hymns 285, 465
    E. "Christian Service in Peru," illustrated with colored slides
    and motion pictures, hymns 118, 17, 515

28 *Youth Sunday*
    M. "Invest Yourself," hymns 60, 300; third annual Everett
    Sunday observance, with pledges and offerings for the work
    of our missionary in Japan, Roy Everett
    E. "Let's Build a New World!" hymns 279, 289, 268

FEBRUARY

 4 Beginning of *Boys' Week*
    M. "The Business of Being a Christian," hymns 533, 232; Boy
    Scouts of Troop 24 as special guests of honor; welcoming of
    February class of new members; broadcast
    E. "The Things That Matter Most," hymns 53, 278, 226

11 *First Sunday in Lent,* "Every Member Present Every Sunday in
    Lent"
    M. "We Believe in Jesus Christ," hymns 1, 140, 142; Communion
    service; February baptismal service
    E. "How to Know God," first of a series of four sermons on
    "Christian Techniques," hymns 166, 242, 142

18 *Second Sunday in Lent*
    M. "Think Magnificently of God," hymns 12, 162
    E. "How to Follow Christ," hymns 232, 149, 261

25 *Third Sunday in Lent, Laymen's Sunday*
   M. "Ordained to Service," hymns 283, 219, with laymen sharing in the service
   E. "How to Read the Bible," hymns 73, 386, 387

MARCH

4 *Fourth Sunday in Lent*
   M. "A Faith That Dares," hymns 372, 256; welcoming of March class of new members; broadcast
   E. "How to Transform One's Life," hymns 245, 231, 337

11 *Passion Sunday, Fifth Sunday in Lent*
   M. "Prayer Releases Power," hymns 261, 243
   E. Lenten drama, presented by the Drama and Pageantry Committee, hymn 95

18 *Palm Sunday, Sixth Sunday in Lent*
   M. "Experiment with Truth," hymns 128, 465; Palm Sunday baptismal service
   E. Oratorio "The Holy City," by Gaul, presented by the Quartet and Chorus Choir

25 *Easter Day*
   M. (two identical services, 9:00 and 11:00 A.M.) "I Too Shall Live!" hymns 154, 150; welcoming of Easter class of new members
   E. "The Afterglow of Easter," hymns 235, 255, 465

APRIL

1 M. "Life Can Be Wonderful," hymns 249, 338; welcoming of April class of new members; broadcast

8 M. "New Accents in Religion," hymns 505, 353; April baptismal service

15 M. "God's Daily Miracles," hymns 18, 210

22 M. "The Challenge of Being a Christian Today," hymns 226, 149

29 M. "God Is Our Refuge and Strength," hymns 315, 321

MAY

6 *Childhood Sunday,* opening *National Family Week*
   M. "Christianity Is like That!" hymns 242, 213; welcoming of May class of new members; broadcast

13 *Mother's Day* (Festival of the Christian Home), *Pentecost*
   M. "The Holy Family," hymns 382, 173; installation of newly
   elected officers of the Woman's Society, the Forty-four Chapter,
   and the Service Guild, all of whom will be guests of honor;
   Mother's Day baptismal service

20 M. "A Look at Your Hands," hymns 165, 387; Communion
   service

27 *Christian Memorial Sunday*
   M. "The Church Triumphant," hymns 334, 515

JUNE

3 M. "What Are You Worth?" hymns 233, 69; welcoming of June
   class of new members; broadcast

10 *Student Day*
   M. "Getting Ready to Live," hymns 435, 446; Student Day
   baptismal service

17 M. "All Things Are Yours!" hymns 120, 234

24 M. "When God Breaks Through," hymns 76, 241

JULY

1 *Independence Sunday*
   M. "Which Way, America?" hymns 491, 489; welcoming of July
   class of new members; broadcast

The remaining morning services of July and August will be
held each Sunday at the usual hour. The sermon subjects and
the names of those preaching will be announced in "The
Visitor" of June 18, which will be the last issue mailed during
the summer. Outstanding soloists of the city will sing during
the summer. Some of these services will be broadcast.

MIDWEEK SERVICES OF PRAYER, BIBLE STUDY, AND FELLOWSHIP

The prime purpose of the midweek church services through
the year will be the deepening and enriching of the Christian
life of the church and of all who attend. Prayer will be a chief
accent, both in the offering of definite prayers for the sick,

troubled, and needy, and in the study of how to pray. Each month will be devoted to a series on the Bible, the church, or some phase of the Christian life. The midweek services are held on Wednesday evenings at 7:30 in the church parlor. During February and March the Wednesday evening services are replaced by the special Lenten services on Thursdays.

SEPTEMBER: How God Helps With—
      6 Our Work
    13 Our Worries and Troubles
    20 Our Failures and Successes
    27 Our Sickness and Health

OCTOBER: Great Eras of the Christian Church
      4 The Church Before the Reformation
    11 The Reformation
    18 The Church in American History
    25 The Church's Chief Tasks Today

NOVEMBER: Great Chapters of the Bible
      1 The Chapter of Faith—Hebrews 11
      8 (The Preaching Mission)
    15 The Chapter of Love—I Corinthians 13
    22 The Chapter of Security—Psalm 23
    29 The Chapter of Abundant Life—Matthew 6

DECEMBER: How to Live an Abundant Christian Life
      6 Expect the Best of Life
    13 Follow the Best in Life
    20 Choose the Noblest from Life
    27 Give Your Best to Life

JANUARY: The Power of Prayer
      3 What Is Prayer?
    10 What Should We Pray For?
    17 Problems of Praying
    24 How God Guides Through Prayer
    31 Ask, and You Shall Receive

APRIL: Little-Known Books of the Old Testament
      4 Jonah—Missions Unlimited

COMMUNION SERVICES

"Do this in remembrance of me" is the invitation-command of the Master to every Christian. The members of our congregation have in large numbers across the years kept their Communion on the sacramental days of the Christian year. The dates set for Communion for the coming year are:

World Communion Sunday, October 1
Watchnight Communion Service, December 31, 11:00 P.M.
Winter Communion Sunday, February 11, first Sunday in Lent
Holy Thursday Candlelight Communion Service, March 22, 8:00 P.M.
Spring Communion Sunday, May 20

Communion cards will be mailed to all members of the church as a reminder of their Christian privilege and duty.

BAPTISMAL SERVICES

The sacrament of Christian baptism will be administered by the ministers at monthly services as follows: the Sunday before

Christmas, Palm Sunday, Mother's Day, Student Day, and in other months the second Sunday.

If the regular services of baptism are inconvenient, or if a time is desired when relatives are in the city, special arrangements will be gladly made by the ministers.

LENTEN SANCTUARY SERVICES COMMITTEE

Across the years your Lenten Sanctuary Services Committee has been extremely successful in maintaining the highest possible standard in the selection of outstanding preachers. That the people of our city appreciate this service is evident both from the large attendance and from the favorable comment concerning the series just closed.

1. The seven dates of this coming Lent will be filled with some of America's most eminent preachers. Their names and dates will be announced as soon as all the invitations have been accepted, probably within the next six weeks.

2. The two services will be held each Thursday of Lent, at 4:00 and at 8:00 P.M., with a special effort to increase the afternoon congregation to the capacity of the sanctuary.

3. The city's best chorus choirs and soloists will be secured to sing for these services.

4. A special newspaper advertisement will announce all seven of the preachers on the Saturday before Lent, with individual pictures and write-ups of each of the guest preachers as they appear, week after week.

5. Radio announcements, new this next year, will be used as an effective form of publicity.

6. Seven thousand Lenten folders will be printed and distributed, as was done this year.

7. Reports of the sermons will be provided for the newspapers for their Friday editions, with an announcement of the next guest preacher.

8. In spite of three blizzards on the first three evenings of this year, the series was financially self-supporting.

BOARD OF EDUCATION

The Board of Education, meeting on the third Wednesday evening of each month, will continue to supervise the entire program of Christian education for children, youth, and adults. The objectives for the coming year will be found under organization and committee reports which follow.

CHURCH SCHOOL

The following are the chief emphases and goals for the year:

1. Growth of Christian character among members of the Church School, with teachers encouraged to secure commitment to Christ and his way of life in every class

2. Increased attendance and membership, with the goal for average attendance set as 525, as compared with the 467 average of the past year

3. Selection of associate teachers for many of the classes

4. Study of new materials and methods by the departmental superintendents, particularly in the Youth Division

5. A new system of records, more complete and more usable than the present system, to go into effect in September

6. Workers' Conferences providing opportunity for discussion of problems and for help and guidance in teaching and organization

7. Increased use of audio-visual materials and methods

8. Missionary education as a regular feature of the Sunday morning program, with the adoption of missionary projects encouraged in all classes

9. Emphasis on stewardship, with all members encouraged to use the envelope system for regular and systematic contributions to the church

10. Training in church membership for sixth graders throughout the year

11. Increased emphasis on music through the three children's choirs in the Kindergarten, Primary, and Junior Departments

12. Increased active co-operation from parents for the various activities of the Children's Division through parent-teacher discussion groups

13. A publicity brochure describing the Church School, to be ready for distribution on Return Sunday

14. Relocation of several departments to give increased efficiency

15. Full co-operation with the City-wide Evangelistic Crusade in November and throughout the year in winning new members to Christ and his church

YOUTH ACTIVITIES

Intermediate Fellowship

The Intermediate Fellowship, composed of seventh and eighth grades, will continue to meet on Sunday afternoons.

1. A regular program of study, including churchmanship, missionary education, and a particular missionary project, will be set up.

2. Increased responsibility for these group activities will be given to the members of the group.

3. Social activities once a month will continue, with the co-operation of parents of members of the group.

High School Fellowship

The High School Fellowship, grades nine through twelve, will continue to meet each Sunday evening with the following schedule:

5:30—informal fellowship and supper preparation
6:30—supper and table recreation
7:30—worship service, followed by discussion of problems selected by the young people

1. The group will take part in the Youth Retreat to be held at Camp Harding, September 15-17.

2. Service to our church will be emphasized, with caroling to shut-in members at Christmas. The young people will assist in any other activity where it is desired.

3. More boxes of clothing will be sent to the family in the Netherlands which the group has assisted during the past year.

4. Increased emphasis on reaching new high school young people will be a definite activity.

5. The fellowship will co-operate with the activities of the Youth Federation of the Federation of Churches.

6. Young people interested in full-time Christian service as a life work will be counseled and encouraged.

7. Social affairs, scheduled according to the needs and interests of the group, will be held.

8. Youth Week will be observed January 28–February 4 with appropriate activities.

Sunday Niters

Young people of college age and above meet together Sunday evenings in an organization called the Sunday Niters. The Steering Committee recommends:

1. A Youth Retreat at Camp Harding, September 15-17

2. A University of Life program on six consecutive Sunday evenings, October 8–November 12

3. Personal contacts inviting students at the schools in our community to participate in the Sunday evening programs and the social activities connected with the Sunday Niters

4. Development of hobby groups in conjunction with the young adult program

AUDIO-VISUAL EDUCATION COMMITTEE

Recognizing the increasing importance of audio-visual methods and materials in Christian education, the committee will continue to seek ways to use our audio-visual equipment more efficiently and effectively.

1. Training classes in the use of equipment will be organized so that more groups in the church may have the benefit of it.

2. Events of importance have been recorded by means of photography during the past year. Many more pictures will be taken during the year to come.

3. A complete pictorial record will be kept of the ground-breaking and subsequent activities connected with the building of the New Edifice.

4. The making of several series of colored slides depicting the activities of the various departments of the Church School is under consideration. It is planned that these series and accompanying scripts will be of educational value to churches other than our own.

5. The purchase of additional equipment, including an opaque projector, is under consideration.

DRAMATICS AND PAGEANTRY COMMITTEE

Dramatics and pageantry, associated traditionally with the church since the Middle Ages, will have an increasing emphasis in the life of our church this year.

1. The committee will be available for consultation and direction by any group in the church interested in play production, stagecraft, or any of the allied arts and crafts.

2. At least two dramatic productions will be staged, a Christmas drama, "A Child Is Born," on Sunday, December 10, and a Lenten drama, to be selected, on Sunday, March 11.

RECREATION AND ATHLETICS COMMITTEE

The committee will continue to co-operate with groups desiring the use of the church recreational facilities. The use of the gymnasium by girls, boys, and young people of the church and community will be continued. Facilities are available for basketball, volleyball, badminton, and table tennis. All activities must be carried on under the supervision of a qualified adult.

MUSIC COMMITTEE

The congregation and the ministers are keenly aware of the high importance of good music in the worship and program of the church. It is believed that the same fine co-operation and excellent teamwork among the director, the organist, the quartet, and the choirs shown this year will make the coming year in music a notable one.

1. A Youth Choir is to be organized among the young people of the church, to sing for their own fellowship services and for the regular church services occasionally.

2. This Youth Choir, the Adult Choir, the Quartet, the Children's Choir, and the Cherub Choir, will be the five chief musical organizations of the church.

3. The first rehearsal of the Adult Choir will be held on Wednesday evening, September 6, singing for the first time in the fall on September 10, and for the last time in the spring on May 27.

4. The Children's Choir plays an important part in the musical religious education program of the girls and boys of the Church School. This group plans to continue to memorize a hymn each month, to learn its origin and meaning, and to sing it from memory on one Sunday morning of the month, except when a children's anthem is substituted for it. The twelve hymns the children will learn are: "My Faith Looks Up to Thee"; "Saviour, Like a Shepherd Lead Us"; "Stand Up, Stand Up for Jesus"; "God Will Take Care of You"; "O Jesus, I Have Promised"; "Take My Life, and Let It Be Consecrated, Lord, to Thee"; "In the Cross of Christ I Glory"; "Rise Up, O Men of God"; "Wonderful Words of Life"; "O Little Town of Bethlehem"; "The Sweet Story of Old"; "Now Thank We All Our God."

5. Outstanding guest soloists will sing at the summer Sunday morning services.

6. Special Christmas music will be presented on Sunday, December 17, and will consist of the choicest of selections of Christmas music. Special Lenten music, "The Holy City" by Gaul, will be presented on Palm Sunday at the evening service.

7. The date of the annual choir party has been set for Tuesday, May 1.

LAY ACTIVITIES COMMITTEE

There has been a renewed interest in cultivating the needs of laymen and of cultivating their interest in working for the total program of the church. We wish to be a part of this progressive movement and recommend:

1. A Laymen's Retreat at Camp Harding, September 9-10

2. A Laymen's Rally, October 15, in preparation for the City-wide Evangelistic Crusade

3. A City-wide Laymen's Communion Breakfast in the spring

4. Observance of Laymen's Sunday, February 25

MEMBERSHIP AND EVANGELISM COMMITTEE

The work of this committee is to recruit, train, and conserve church members. Winning people to Christ and assimilating them in the program of the Christian church are the first concerns of this committee. We recommend:

1. A goal of two hundred new members to be received during the year

2. Participation in the City-wide Evangelistic Crusade, November 5-12

3. Continuation of The Seventy (composed of thirty-five teams of two, organized into seven groups, with a captain for each group) to make monthly calls on prospective new members, with dinner meetings for fellowship and instruction on September 12 and January 10

4. A four-month training period for boys and girls to be received into membership on Sunday, April 29

5. Reception of new members on the first Sunday of each month, and other Sundays as arranged by the minister

6. Co-operation with the Church School and other groups in securing commitment to Christ and the Christian way of life

7. A class for instruction of new members received either on confession of faith or by transfer

8. Election of a church membership secretary

9. Continued use of every present method of winning people, including: calls on new residents of the city; contacts with the Y.M.C.A. and Y.W.C.A.; Thanksgiving, Christmas, and Easter folders; and emphasis on visitation during the Lenten season

FLOWER AND DECORATIONS COMMITTEE

Each Sunday the chancel flowers are for the most part presented as memorials to departed loved ones. These flowers represent both a tribute to those who have passed on and a service to the church that enriches the spirit of worship.

While thirty-seven of the Sundays of the year are already spoken for, the other fifteen may be had by any who desire them. They are: the first Sunday in September; the first and third in October; the first in November; the third and fourth in January; the first in March; the last in June; all four in July; and the first, third, and fourth in August.

The decorations on certain special Sundays will be cared for by the following classes: Thanksgiving Sunday, Partnership Class; Christmas Sunday, Married Couples Class; Palm Sunday and Easter, Mr. and Mrs. Class; Mother's Day, Fifty-Fifty Class; Student Day, Youth Fellowships.

USHERS AND COLLECTORS COMMITTEE

The ushers and collectors are in a special sense "public relations representatives" in promoting the spirit of friendliness and reverence at all the services of the church.

1. The plan of having sixty ushers, divided into groups of ten, with each usher serving for a period of two months, as started last March, will be continued through the year, under the direction of the committee. The names of those ushering will appear each week in "The Visitor."

2. The application of this same principle to the task of the collectors will be considered in the autumn.

3. Because our church is so well filled practically every Sunday morning, the ushers will try to secure the co-operation of every member in the seating of as many people as possible.

4. A list of "Suggestions to Ushers," which grew out of their own discussion of their task and opportunities, will be placed in the hands of all ushers.

FINANCE COMMITTEE

For more than a quarter of a century our members have been known as glad and generous givers, who pay as they pledge. This year 1,178 members or couples pledged a total of over $55,000, the largest amount in a great many years.

1. On Loyalty Sunday, October 15, members will be urged to bring their pledges to the current-expense and benevolent budgets to the services of worship. Those not pledging in this manner will be visited in their homes.

2. At the end of each three-month period Quarterly Settlement Reminders will be sent to each subscriber.

3. A pledge card with a package of offering envelopes will be sent to every new member with a letter or by a personal visit immediately after he joins the church.

4. Special offerings on Thanksgiving, Christmas, and Easter will be received.

5. The educationally sound practice of encouraging the children of the Church School to make a pledge to their church on Loyalty Sunday and to use offering envelopes will be continued.

6. The practice of Christian stewardship in systematic giving will be commended from time to time.

BUILDING COMMITTEE

Among the events that have indicated progress in the unfolding of the building enterprise during the past year are the following:

1. An additional lot was purchased, enabling the church to locate the New Edifice far more advantageously as well as to provide more space for parking and gardens.

2. The architect was authorized to proceed with working drawings, after the floor plans are finally determined, so that bids can be secured from building concerns.

The coming year will be in some regards an even more important one, as the floor plans will be finally decided on, the working drawings will be completed, and the plans submitted to building contractors for bids.

ENDOWMENT COMMITTEE

The only justification for the acquisition of property beyond the supplying of our own physical needs is that it may be used for the development of spiritual values. The rich farmer, prototype of all men of narrow acquisitive instincts, whose entire horizon embraced only the building of larger barns to hold larger harvests, merited the condemnation, "Thou fool! this night thy soul shall be required of thee." How best can our money be used to promote spiritual values? By providing that it should be wisely used by experienced people interested in promoting the general good. That can be done for you by entrusting part of it to your church to use after you are gone.

A gift to the Endowment Fund of your church for God's use is one of the best ways to accomplish this end. Consult your pastor or any member of the Endowment Committee about how it can be done. It deserves your careful and prayerful thought and planning.

PUBLIC RELATIONS COMMITTEE

A well-rounded program of planned publicity can be of great value to any church, especially one like ours that has so many events of interest to the general public. With the public press so friendly and generous to the churches, every organization in the church should have an active publicity committee to send frequent articles to the newspaper.

1. All the regular types of publicity, such as paid newspaper advertising, hotel bulletin board announcements, Christmas and Easter folders, announcement of the hours of service in the daily papers, and general news articles, with pictures where possible, will be continued and expanded.

2. The size and the name of "The Visitor" will be studied, with the possibility that they might be changed when the church occupies the New Edifice. Also the use of color in paper or printers' ink will be investigated.

3. An airplane picture of the New Site will be taken and used where desired.

4. A letter will be sent late in August to the heads of all church organizations, urging them that they appoint a Public Relations Committee of three members at once; and a meeting of all these committees will be held on Sunday, September 10, to discuss the best ways of giving publicity to events. Pamphlets on the subject will be given out, if any can be secured.

5. Members of the congregation will be invited to coin an appropriate descriptive title for our church, such as, "The Friendly Church," or "The City-wide Family Church," and send it to the committee.

6. Any historic event or anniversary during the year will be featured with an article and picture.

7. The larger organizations of the church, such as the Church School, the Woman's Society, and the Youth Groups, will be given prominence in "The Visitor" by the use of an extra insert page from time to time.

8. An attractive church sign will be placed on the lawn of the New Site, that people may know the location of our new church home.

9. Members will be urged to share in a campaign of "personal publicity" by making the church the topic of conversation with their friends, and some layman will present this suggestion to the congregation on a Sunday morning in September.

10. The committee will invite the church editors of our local newspapers to a luncheon to secure from them suggestions for better public relations.

11. Members will be urged to give a friendly greeting to those in near-by pews at the close of the services each Sunday.

12. The committee will investigate any other promising avenues of publicity.

RADIO COMMITTEE

The outreach of our ministry of worship and service has across the past eighteen years been greatly extended by radio broadcasts on the first Sunday of each month, as well as additional Sundays during the summer.

1. Services will be broadcast this summer on the first and fourth Sundays of June; the first, third, and fourth Sundays in July; and the first, third, and fourth Sundays in August.

2. The field of television will be studied by the committee during the year to discover what the future may hold for the televising of church services.

3. A radio-television room or booth is being included in the plans for the sanctuary of the New Edifice.

FELLOWSHIP FAMILY NIGHT COMMITTEE

Family dinners for fellowship and inspiration have proved their value in emphasizing the relation of church and family and the importance of each for the other. Children, youth, and adults have been so enthusiastic about them that the committee plans to increase their number to nine, one each month during the autumn, winter, and spring. The program of each dinner will be planned to serve some need of the families of the church and to promote friendship.

1. The dates proposed for the Fellowship Family Nights are: October 6, November 3, December 8, January 5, February 2, March 2, April 6, May 11 (National Family Week), June 8.

2. The Board of Missions will sponsor the October 6 dinner as a great welcome back to Dr. and Mrs. Joe Winthrop by the families of the church.

3. The Church School will sponsor the December 8 dinner as a Sunday School Christmas Party.

BOARD OF MISSIONS

The board looks forward to a year in which we all become personally better acquainted with our missionaries and the work they are doing. This personal contact will be extended to the entire congregation through a more intensive educational program starting in the autumn. The missionaries now being supported in part or entirely by our church are:

> Rev. Joseph Winthrop, China
> Rev. Arthur L. Flagg, India
> Rev. Henry E. Pullen, Africa
> Rev. John H. Tobin, Peru
> Rev. Edward M. Winter, Hawaii
> Rev. Roy Everett, Japan

1. A World Vision Fellowship Family Night will be held on Friday evening, October 6, with Dr. and Mrs. Winthrop as speakers and guests of honor. They expect to return to the United States in August. Chinese students attending local educational institutions will be invited. Dr. Winthrop will share the pulpit on October 8 at the morning and evening services.

2. John Tobin will return from Peru for his year in the United States sometime next spring and will visit us. Plans will be made as soon as his schedule is known.

3. A portrait photograph of each of our missionaries whose picture we do not now have will be procured by autumn, as well as more snapshots of work they are doing. Films will be sent them when the size of their cameras is known. Cuts will be made from these photographs of each of our missionaries, to be put in folder form and to be used in "The Visitor" with letters or articles which they may send from time to time.

4. A folder on some phase of home or foreign missions will be distributed to the congregation at the Sunday services about once each month.

5. The fourth Sunday of each month will continue to be observed as World Vision Sunday in the Church School, with the entire offering being contributed for missions and related causes. Plans are being made in co-operation with the Board of Education for each department of the Church School to "adopt" and contribute to the support of a mission child of appropriate age.

GOOD LITERATURE COMMITTEE

A well-informed Christian will be a better Christian. A vast wealth of good religious literature is available in pamphlets, books, and periodicals, which should be read by more and more church members. The following program is planned:

1. Continued promotion of daily devotional literature for personal and family devotions, with special distribution to all who are ill or shut-in

2. Securing of subscriptions to our denominational papers in increasingly large numbers of our homes

3. Continuation of six months gift subscriptions for new members of the church

4. Publication in "The Visitor" each month of two or three

titles of religious books recommended by the ministers, these books to be displayed on a literature table for examination and purchase

5. Development of plans for wider use and enlargement of our Church School library

6. Distribution of free leaflets as they may be available

7. Observance of Universal Bible Sunday on December 10

8. Co-operation with the Federation of Churches, where possible, in literature distribution to the hospitals and institutions of our city

CHURCH HISTORICAL COMMITTEE

Special recommendations of this committee are:

1. To microfilm newspaper articles and other similar materials during the year so that they may be retained for permanent use

2. If financially possible, to microfilm all of the material stored in the safe, both to provide a permanent record and to make these materials available for film slides

3. To secure more information about the earlier churches of our city

4. To dramatize some of the historical events in co-operation with the Audio-Visual Education and the Dramatics and Pageantry Committees

WOMAN'S SOCIETY

The Woman's Society is one of the major organizations of our church. Women from all walks of life are attracted to it because of the wide scope of its programs, a few of which are: home and family life; community, state, national, and international problems; alcohol; interracial relations; and home and foreign missions.

The circles have been reorganized, now numbering ten, each with a program and definite purpose. All circle meetings are held the fourth Tuesday of each month for program and sewing or special work. The general meetings of the society are held on the second Tuesday of each month, with a luncheon at 12:30 followed by the business meeting and program. No meetings are held in July and August.

A retreat is being planned for September. Woman's Society Sunday will be observed December 17, with Mrs. J. D. Welcombe as guest speaker.

The executive board of the Woman's Society hopes to attain the national goals of new members, better educational programs, increased giving, and recruits to full-time Christian service. The study topics for the new year are: "Mohammedanism Today," "Building a Christian Community," "Worship," and "Christian Vocations."

FORTY-FOUR CHAPTER

The Forty-Four Chapter is composed of a group of mothers who because of small children are unable to attend afternoon meetings of the Woman's Society. A dinner meeting at 6:45 P.M. followed by a program and business meeting is held the fourth Tuesday of the month. Plans for this year include:

1. Continued support of the work in China of Miss Mary Fletcher and Miss Jane Barber, as well as other projects in the mission field

2. Proceeds from rummage sales and other projects to be added to the Susan Anderson Memorial, a scholarship fund established for the use of young people who are entering full-time Christian service

3. Supplying the Webster Children's Home with clothing and other articles needed

4. Continued meeting of the neighborhood work groups on any project that the chapter may sponsor to benefit the church and Woman's Society work

SERVICE GUILD

The Service Guild is an international organization for business and professional women. Through its program of world brotherhood, Christian social relations, local church activities, and enrichment of spiritual life its goal is to help gainfully employed women to find fellowship and constructive living in the Christian way of life. Among the objectives for the year are:

1. The promotion of happy and helpful friendships among the business and professional women of our church

2. The enlistment of a larger number of new members so that the Guild may reach more of the employed women of the city

3. The interesting of many younger employed women in the program of service and fellowship of the Guild

4. The giving of as much as possible to the many worthy projects of the Guild

5. The repetition of our gift of one hundred dollars toward the support of our missionary in Japan, Roy Everett

BOYS' WORK COMMITTEE

1. A complete record on every boy, giving full information on his participation in the church and community program, is to be compiled in conjunction with the new record system being worked out by the Church School.

2. We will continue to sponsor Boy Scout Troop 24.

3. Members of the Scout Committee will keep in touch with eleven-year-old boys and introduce them to a Scout troop in the city.

4. The gymnasium will be available to boys under proper supervision.

5. The annual Father and Son Banquet will be held Friday evening, April 13.

6. This committee is responsible for boys only through high

school and recommends that a special committee be appointed to keep in touch with older boys and young men up through their early twenties. This might well be carried on as a part of the youth program.

7. The committee will investigate the possibilities of organizing a Cub Scout pack among the younger boys of our church.

GREETERS COMMITTEE

Our church should be known by everyone as "The Friendly Church." It is now so known by many people, but greater effort should be made to develop that family spirit which makes every member feel at home. Because it is the privilege of every member to express the spirit of Christian friendship in every relation of life, especially in the church, we recommend:

1. Continuation of placing "greeters" at the church door at the close of the service to shake hands and pass a friendly word with those who attend

2. Placing a "greeter" at the church door before the morning service to supply information and assistance

3. A meeting of this committee with the Ushers' Committee to see wherein we can supplement the work of the ushers and help to avoid unnecessary duplication and overlapping of duties

4. Periodic announcements from the pulpit of the work of the committee, with the recommendation that the greeting be done by all worshipers at the close of the service

5. A guest book supplementing the registration card system, with announcements from the pulpit and in "The Visitor" to stimulate its use

6. A floor plan of the existing church building in sketch form for circulation to aid newcomers in finding their way about

7. A special "greeters" corps to be assigned to welcome each class of new members

NEW MEMBERS ACQUAINTANCE COMMITTEE

For several years this committee has been responsible for a dinner or reception given in the spring to new members.

1. On Friday evening, October 20, a fall reception for new members will be held. Invitations will be mailed. Each class and organization will be requested to have several members present. A small brochure giving full information about our church program will be distributed at the reception.

2. The committee will meet later for evaluating the reception and making plans for the next social occasion.

CHRISTIAN STEWARDSHIP COMMITTEE

1. Stewardship Sunday will be observed on October 22, the program to be devoted to an exposition and explanation of stewardship in its broadest sense. Cards are to be distributed and filled out at this service. The committee will follow up the information obtained from these cards.

2. The theme of the Youth Retreat at Camp Harding, September 15-17, will be the influence of the Christian faith in choosing one's life vocation, and the committee will co-operate in this program.

3. Stewardship literature, including a definition of stewardship, will be presented in the form of a number of brief articles in "The Visitor."

CO-OPERATION COMMITTEE

The responsibility of this committee is to seek co-operation with other churches and constructive agencies and groups in the community. We recommend:

1. Continued co-operation with other churches and Christian agencies of the city through the Federation of Churches, the Council of Church Women, the Youth Federation, the Allied Temperance Forces, and the Inter-Faith Committee

2. Inclusion of these groups as well as the State Council of Churches, the National Council of Churches, and the World Council of Churches, in our annual budget, as is our custom

3. A service in recognition of the National Council of the Churches of Christ in the U.S.A. on Sunday, December 3

CHRISTIAN SOCIAL ACTION COMMITTEE

The chief purpose of this committee is to study and to recommend ways in which the principles of our Christian religion can be applied to the civic, moral, and social problems that confront our community, our nation, and our world. The committee proposes:

1. To continue its study of the features of an over-all program of information, discussion, and action suited to the needs of our church

2. To encourage every member of the church to realize that it is his Christian responsibility and duty to participate actively in civic, educational, social, and governmental matters, especially by voting in every primary and regular election

3. To furnish guidance through pamphlets and literature and through short articles in "The Visitor" on matters that come within the scope of the duty of this committee

4. To foster a sense of individual responsibility for the operation of our government in accord with Christian principles

5. To encourage the registration of every qualified member of the church so that he may vote

6. To encourage free discussion of social and moral problems through the various organizations and classes of the church

SOCIAL SERVICE AND LOCAL RELIEF COMMITTEE

So far as funds are available this committee will give temporary or emergency assistance to those in need. The names of those receiving aid will always be kept in strict confidence. We propose:

1. Sending Thanksgiving and Christmas baskets to needy families as heretofore

2. Securing information from all organizations of the church to discover what social needs are being met in our church and community, and recommending that each group accept some definite social responsibility

3. Contact with our members in homes and institutions to make sure that their major needs are being cared for

VISITATION AND PARISH GROUP COMMITTEE

In a large city-wide family church like ours there is real need for those members living in the same locality to become acquainted with each other. The Parish Group Plan of several years ago, which divided the church membership into about 130 geographical groups, is now being reorganized, and members are being assigned to the parish group in which they reside for acquaintance and fellowship and calling by the parish group leader. New members received during the year will be added to the proper groups. The program of calling for the year involves two church-wide calls, as follows:

1. The autumn call, during the week beginning Sunday, September 24, is for the purposes of becoming acquainted; of inviting every member to take Communion on October 1, World Communion Sunday; and of urging attendance at church every Sunday through October, which is Church Loyalty Month. Pamphlets about the work of the church will be left in each home.

2. The Lenten call, during the week beginning Sunday, February 4, is for the purposes of securing promises of all members to attend church all the Sundays in Lent; of urging general attendance at the seven Lenten sanctuary services on Thursday; and of "keeping Lent" in the spirit of Christ.

HOSPITALS AND HOMES COMMITTEE

For a number of years our members have contributed generously to the support of the Grace Hospital charity ward and the Webster Children's Home. For continued vigorous support we recommend:

1. Inclusion of a substantial contribution to Grace Hospital in the budget for the new year

2. Assignment of the entire special Christmas offering to the Webster Children's Home

3. Suggestions to classes in the Church School and other groups of special projects to be undertaken for these institutions and of visits to them whenever possible

"THE VISITOR" COMMITTEE

"The Visitor" brings to the church members each week the program of the church services, including its various organizations. It endeavors to present the numerous activities, as well as other items of importance to members and friends, in an interesting and newsy manner.

Twenty-four hundred "Visitors" will be printed each Wednesday from September 6 to June 20. Somewhat over three fourths will be mailed to our constituency, the rest handed out at the morning and evening services.

In addition to supplying our people with the program of our church "The Visitor" also will contain matter relating to the church at large, and from time to time letters and information concerning our ministers and workers abroad. Several of the committees have recommended that "The Visitor" should endeavor to present such topics as stewardship, missions, and the co-operative task of the church.

INDEX

Numbers in italic type refer to specimen reports in the Appendix.

Date Due